Understanding the Markets

Butterworth-Heinemann – The Securities Institute

A publishing partnership

About The Securities Institute

Formed in 1992 with the support of the Bank of England, the London Stock Exchange, the Financial Services Authority, LIFFE and other leading financial organizations, the Securities Institute is the professional body for practitioners working in securities, investment management, corporate finance, derivatives and related businesses. Their purpose is to set and maintain professional standards through membership, qualifications, training and continuing learning and publications. The Institute promotes excellence in matters of integrity, ethics and competence.

About the series

Butterworth-Heinemann is pleased to be the official **Publishing Partner** of the Securities Institute with the development of professional level books for: Brokers/Traders; Actuaries; Consultants; Asset Managers; Regulators; Central Bankers; Treasury Officials; Compliance Officers; Legal Departments; Corporate Treasurers; Operations Managers; Portfolio Managers; Investment Bankers; Hedge Fund Managers; Investment Managers; Analysts and Internal Auditors, in the areas of: Portfolio Management; Advanced Investment Management; Investment Management Models; Financial Analysis; Risk Analysis and Management; Capital Markets; Bonds; Gilts; Swaps; Repos; Futures; Options; Foreign Exchange; Treasury Operations.

Series titles

- **Professional Reference Series**
  The Bond and Money Markets: *Strategy, Trading, Analysis*

- **Global Capital Markets Series**
  The REPO Handbook
  Foreign Exchange and Money Markets: *Theory, Practice and Risk Management*
  IPO and Equity Offerings
  European Securities Markets Infrastructure
  Best Execution in the Integrated Securities Market

- **Operations Management Series**
  Clearing, Settlement and Custody
  Controls, Procedures and Risks
  Relationship and Resource Management in Operations
  Managing Technology in the Operations Function
  Regulation and Compliance in Operations
  Understanding the Markets

For more information

For more information on **The Securities Institute** please visit their web site:

www.securities-institute.org.uk

and for details of all **Butterworth-Heinemann Finance** titles please visit Butterworth-Heinemann:

www.bh.com/finance

Understanding the Markets

David Loader

OXFORD AMSTERDAM BOSTON LONDON NEW YORK PARIS
SAN DIEGO SAN FRANCISCO SINGAPORE SYDNEY TOKYO

Butterworth-Heinemann
An imprint of Elsevier Science
Linacre House, Jordan Hill, Oxford OX2 8DP
225 Wildwood Avenue, Woburn, MA 01801-2041

First published 2002

British Library Cataloguing in Publication Data
A catalogue record for this book is available from the British Library

Library of Congress Cataloguing in Publication Data
A catalogue record for this book is available from the Library of Congress

ISBN 0 7506 5465 1

Composition by Genesis Typesetting, Rochester, Kent
Printed and bound in Great Britain by Biddles Ltd, *www.biddles.co.uk*

Contents

Preface

The financial markets have undergone massive changes over the centuries that business, commerce, trading and finance have been part of life. That change accelerated through the latter part of the twentieth century and continues today. Considering that everything which occurs in the financial markets has an effect on us all, the actual workings of the financial markets remain to many somewhat of a mystery.

As a result, not only those who rely on them for their savings and investments but also those who work within the industry perhaps misunderstand the markets. This book can only scratch the surface of what is a massive industry, which is truly global and very diverse, to provide an insight into the way in which parts of the financial markets work. It will also look at the markets from the viewpoint of the person working in the operations functions that support the trading, dealing and investment processes.

It is important to understand the enormity of the industry. We are not just talking about statistics and mind-boggling monetary amounts, we are looking at an industry that drives the fundamentals of world trade and one that, of course, generates wealth. It reaches every corner of the world with markets for food, natural resources, property, manufacturing and financial services in every country. Inevitably politics and opinion are robustly influential. Economies of the world have so much interaction that many markets are not purely domestic and move in accordance with international demand and whims. The US economy and those of the major developed countries do influence other markets and economies, sometimes with what is perceived to be a negative impact.

As a result, since the last decade of the twentieth century London and other major financial centres have suffered disruption, rioting, vandalism and crime by various groups opposed to the globalization of markets, the enormous gap between the rich, developed countries and the struggling Third World and capitalism in general. Their arguments may well have merit but their attempts to 'Stop the City' (as the action is called when it takes place in London) were never likely to succeed and also ignored many highly significant issues supporting the argument that capitalism works. This book is not about the pros and cons of capitalism. However, what the attacks on the City of London and elsewhere, if that it is not too emotive, do illustrate is the importance of these financial centres. Clearly the demonstrators felt the need to target London and it was unlikely to have been because they considered it a soft touch. They wanted to make their point somewhere that was relevant.

So is London really a major financial market and if so, why and will it remain that way? What are the other main financial centres and how do they differ?

Statistics tell many stories and these are presented elsewhere in this book. However, one major reason that London is still very much a leading financial centre is because there is a wealth of skilled people able to support an increasingly diverse, innovative and global market. We should also acknowledge that London is historically a financial centre and is ideally situated between the US and Asian markets. It has a reasonably business-friendly regulatory environment and employment laws, and yet it is certain that it is the skills and knowledge and quality of the people which play a significant part in making London successful as a financial centre. I hasten to add that other centres like New York, Tokyo, Frankfurt and Zurich all have various reasons for their success as financial centres. Markets are where the business is and whether it is for historical reasons, infrastructure, tax advantages (hence there are offshore centres like the Channel Islands, Bermuda and Dublin), workforce skills or any combination of these, a market is successful because it serves the business. It is nevertheless my view that it is the skills of the people working in and supporting the financial markets that is the key to ultimate success.

Those skills are spread across dealing, corporate finance, information technology and operations. Some would argue that financial markets today are becoming so automated that it is possible to place a dealing team anywhere in the world where they can connect to the network and trading systems. The advent of Internet trading supports this, so does the remote access afforded by some electronic exchanges. The dealers do not have to be where the exchange is but this is hardly new.

The foreign exchange market has always been telephone-based enabling trading in currencies 24 hours a day, 365 days a year, but then

Global foreign exchange market turnover (daily averages in April, in billions of US dollars)[1]

Instrument	*1989*	*1992*	*1995*	*1998*[2]	*2001*
Spot transactions	317	394	494	568	387
Outright forwards	27	58	97	128	131
Foreign exchange swaps	190	324	546	734	656
Total 'traditional' turnover	**590**	**820**	**1190**	**1490**	**1210**
Memorandum item:					
Turnover at April 2001 exchange rates[3]	570	750	990	1400	1210

[1] Adjusted for local and cross-border double-counting.
[2] Revised.
[3] Non-US dollar legs of foreign currency transactions were converted into original currency amounts at average exchange rates for April of each survey year and then reconverted into US dollar amounts at average April 2001 exchange rates.
Source: Bank for International Settlements.

there is no physical marketplace. The foreign exchange markets support arguments about financial centres being where the business is, London being the world's leading centre for foreign exchange trading, and yet much of that business originates from outside the UK.

The London Stock Exchange is the largest in Europe but it is not the oldest. New York boasts the world's largest stock market. Chicago has the largest US derivatives exchanges. Frankfurt is home to the world's second largest derivatives exchange and yet only a few years ago there was no derivative exchange there at all and London dominated financial futures and options trading in Europe. If Frankfurt has the second largest derivatives market where is the largest? Why is Lloyd's of London the pre-eminent insurance market in the world? Where is the centre for gold trading? Why did the stock and derivatives markets in Hong Kong and Singapore feel the need to merge? Why did Paris, Brussels and Amsterdam do the same thing with Lisbon following suit in 2002?

These are interesting questions, and important ones too. So what are the reasons for markets being where they are and what are the drivers behind change in the financial markets?

Markets undergo change in just the same way as everything else. Bartering gave way to cash, which gave way to credit. Specialist shops gave way to supermarkets so that choice was increased and prices were reduced (in theory anyway). Manufacturing and heavy industry went where labour was cheapest, which is why a piece of electrical equipment that has travelled half-way round the world to be sold in a British shop is still cheaper than if it had been made in the UK. Financial markets went where the business was most competitive and the administration of the business was of the best quality.

Today the markets are again subject to much change: mergers, alliances even take-overs as exchanges convert from being mutual societies (owned by members) to publicly quoted companies owned by shareholders. The change is driven by many factors but the power of the users of markets is significant. Users of markets like banks, brokers, fund managers and corporate businesses have experienced and are still undergoing massive change themselves.

This is largely as a result of deregulation of the markets, allowing organizations to become multi-product businesses and also because of the need for enormous scale to generate levels of business that can make a profit and can service an increasingly sophisticated and global client base. The rise of the global investment bank has led to many established businesses being swallowed up so that, oddly, a major financial centre like London is home today to a multitude of foreign-owned banks and brokers and, increasingly, fund managers. In financial markets at least big is indeed beautiful but equally there is still undoubtedly a role for the niche players. There is also increasing concern that the really large firms, banks, brokers or corporate businesses are so large that controlling the business becomes difficult, sometimes with disastrous consequences as recent events at Enron and Allied Irish Bank's US offshoot demonstrate.

As the markets undergo change so too do the administration, clearing and settlement functions as the clearing houses, securities depositories and custodians merge and diversify. This, of course, is going to impact on the operations teams that support the trading, sales and retail business. A failure to be aware of and understand the impact of changes in the markets will create massive problems, greater risk and ultimately financial losses. And yet the sheer size and diversity of the global markets, together with the pace of change, expansion and increasing volumes of transactions needing to be processed, presents a massive challenge to the operations teams and managers.

The importance of technology in all of this is somewhat obvious as none of it would be remotely possible if it were not for advances in this field. However, technology can be a potential problem when it comes to operations, not because the clearing houses have not developed new systems to cope with the changes in the market, because they have. It is because for the basic systems used for administration and accounting in the organizations operating in the markets, the upgrading and introduction of new systems takes longer, is more problematic in implementation and is often highly expensive.

For operations then the markets are king. They generate the business that justifies the existence of operations and also some at least of the problems that need to be dealt with. The markets are complex, innovative and, above all, changing. Knowing how the markets work and what impacts on the operations team is crucial for managers and supervisors. In this book we try to rise to the challenge of explaining markets and their influence in operations terms so that if you are about to embark on a career in operations it should be very useful. If you are planning a career as a dealer it will prove essential if only to explain that something happens after you have traded.

Chapter 1

Introduction

We refer to the 'markets' or 'the capital markets' or the 'City' or indeed many other such generic expressions in business, in the media or in general conversation, but what exactly do we mean?

'The markets' can mean stocks or shares, or money or commodities or, for that matter, commerce. A livestock farmer probably relates the term 'market' to something quite different from a banker, likewise estate agents and fund managers, yet the 'financial' markets affect them all in some way or other. On that basis markets are perhaps best described as component parts of the business and commerce functions that exist within the economic environment of a country.

In the financial services industry such markets exist in a variety of guises. We have stock markets, money markets, derivative markets, commodity markets and also wholesale and retail markets. In many instances there is a direct relationship between them so that investment products sold in the retail markets are structured around products traded in, for instance, the stock markets. This interaction is crucial as, for instance, the fundamental function of a stock market is to enable companies to raise finance and this relies on investors providing the finance through direct (purchase of shares) or indirect (purchase of investment products, e.g. ISAs) buying of the stock offered. We can also look at house buyers in the 'property market' who, in most cases, need to raise funding through mortgages or loans from banks. The property market reacts to the availability of the buyers, who react to the ability to raise mortgages. In turn this is dependent on issues such as interest rates, the employment outlook, house prices, etc.

It is this complexity of users and products and 'markets' that makes for what is often viewed by the public as a different and daunting world. In reality that is not the case, certainly in terms of the basic structure of the financial markets. It is essentially a very straightforward situation. Capital markets provide the means to raise funds and to gain a return on an investment. So on that basic premise the various 'markets' and 'participants' are users and or providers in the process. Before the deregulation of the UK financial markets in 1995, the participants were clearly defined. Brokers and banks and building societies, for instance, were separate businesses. Merchant banks were different from retail or high street banks. Fund managers were separate from banks.

Following the 'big bang' (as it was called) any organization could operate in any area. So we had the creation of 'investment banks' providing a wide variety of retail and merchant banking, fund management and broking services. Banks started offering mortgages and building societies other types of banking services. Business grew and as the demand for retail and commercial products increased so did the sophistication of the participants, the products and the services offered. This in turn led to the globalization of the financial markets as overseas banks took stakes in banks and brokers in the UK, and subsequently other countries, as they deregulated their markets and as investment products began to trade cross-border in terms of investments and retail selling.

Today the financial or capital markets are performing essentially the same fundamental role as centuries ago. What is significantly different, however, is the speed of the process, the international nature of investment business, the complexity of deals to meet the sophistication of the users' requirements and the sheer size of the 'market'. We can also ponder the by-products of this such as risk and crime, which are and always have been important issues. The regulation of today's markets is far greater than that of even 50 years ago. Criminal acts such as fraud are today supplemented by more sinister crimes like money laundering.

In a hugely competitive environment the investing public is greatly at risk from hard selling, mis-selling (e.g. pensions), and having their money and assets put at unacceptable risk. The authorities have responded accordingly and not just to protect the private investor. Following widely reported industry 'disasters' where large and small organizations have made massive and sometimes fatal losses, the danger to the whole industry of the inability to recognize and control risk in financial markets activities has, to some extent, been addressed. Measures such as capital requirements for banks to mitigate against the market, counterparty and, more recently, operational risk generated by their activities and exposures to products and counterparties have been introduced. It is a far cry from the days of 'my word is my bond', a traditional underpinning of the London stock market, but then today's market culture bears no resemblance to those of yesteryear.

Another major factor in the development of the markets we operate in today has been the advance of technology. Paper has given way to systems and electronic transfer of data. It has also changed markets themselves as many exchanges have moved from the traditional face-to-face trading to electronic trading. The single biggest impact of this change has been on capacity. With so much paper and manual processes involved in trading and settlement of UK equity business, the whole process was grinding to a halt as a transaction took weeks and even months to settle while the paperwork flowed back and forth between client, broker and registrar. With the scenario further complicated every time there was a corporate action coupled with longer and longer claims chains it was little wonder that securities business could not grow and, worse, investors at home and abroad began to look elsewhere to invest and list their shares.

The London Stock Exchange, aware of the problem and most of the source of the problem, began the process of moving towards more automated settlement processes, which culminated with the formation of CREST in 1994 and the introduction of dematerialized, book entry transfer settlement of equity transactions, although the option still to have a share certificate was retained. Today dematerialized settlement exists in many of the major and not so major markets and so too does rolling settlement. Rolling settlement, whereby a trade settles *X* number of days after trade date, has replaced the traditional period settlement, known as 'account settlement'. In the UK this was a process where all the trades completed within an 'account period' usually of two weeks, settled on the same day, or at least were due to. In France there was a monthly settlement period.

In the late 1990s an example of the speed of change induced by technology occurred in derivative markets. The largest markets were

Figure 1.1 LIFFE's old trading floor – Cannon Bridge, London

in Chicago and London which were open-outcry markets where boys and girls in multi-coloured jackets shouted and gesticulated at each other in often frantic trading (see Figure 1.1). So sure of the merits of open-outcry were the London International Financial Futures and Options Exchange (LIFFE) that they had purchased a site at Spitalfields in London to build a large new trading floor. And yet in Frankfurt a wholly electronic derivatives market, the Deutsche Terminborse (DTB), had quietly been building up its volume and, more importantly, gaining an increasing share of the volume in the German Bund futures contract at the expense of LIFFE. One reason was that dealers liked the flexibility of remote dealing from an office rather than on an exchange floor and also, crucially, it was a lot cheaper than maintaining expensive floor teams.

Worse was to come for LIFFE when the DTB and the Swiss Options and Financial Futures Exchange (SOFFEX) joined forces to form EUREX, creating diversity and even greater participation. As the loss of business in its flagship contract gathered momentum it quickly became unstoppable and from one fleeting but glorious month of being the world's busiest derivatives exchange, LIFFE was brought to its knees and forced to abandon its grand plans for the Spitalfields site and belatedly grasp the nettle of developing an electronic trading system for the exchange. The LIFFE floor eventually closed but happily for the exchange their electronic trading system, CONNECT, has proved highly successful and the trading volumes have grown again, particularly in the interest rate futures and options contracts. Today LIFFE is part of the EURONEXT grouping of exchanges and is once again a leading derivatives market, but it was a close thing. Table 1.1 shows the electronic and open-outcry markets as of the beginning of 2002.

Technology in the form of Internet dealing, intranets and online banking has also revolutionized the way in which people use the financial markets and how others in the markets respond. The rise and sometimes just as rapid fall of the day trader, hedge funds, dotcom companies etc. created new organizations, new products,

Table 1.1 Electronic and open-outcry markets (2002)

Exchange	Type	Electronic dealing system	Trading floor
London Stock Exchange	Securities	Stock Exchange Electronic Trading System (SETS) Stock Exchange Automated Quote System (SEAQ)	No
London International Financial Futures and Options Exchange	Financial and commodity derivatives	LIFFE CONNECT	No
New York Stock Exchange	Securities	SuperDot (order system) Broker Booth Support System	Twenty trading posts manned by a specialist around which orders are traded
Chicago Board of Trade	Financial and commodity derivatives	a/c/e (alliance/ CBOT®/Eurex) electronic trading platform	Trading pits (designated trading areas)
Chicago Mercantile Exchange	Financial and commodity derivatives	Globex (20% of the exchange volume in 2001)	Trading pits (designated trading areas)
EURONEXT	Securities and derivatives	Securities – NSC cross-border trading system Derivatives – will adopt LIFFE CONNECT	No

Table 1.1 Continued

Exchange	Type	Electronic dealing system	Trading floor
Eurex	Financial and commodity derivatives	Computerized Eurex Platform	No
Deutsche Borse	Securities	Xetra	No
Tokyo Stock Exchange	Securities, financial derivatives	Computer-assisted Order Routing and Execution System (CORES)	No
SGX Singapore Exchanges	Securities, financial and commodity derivatives	Electronic Trading System for some derivatives	Yes for some derivatives
Australian Stock Exchange	Securities and derivatives	Stock Exchange Automated Trading System (SEATS)	No
Sydney Futures Exchange	Financial and commodity derivatives	Fully electronic, 24-hour system	No
Hong Kong Exchanges & Clearing	Securities and derivatives	Securities – via terminals in the Exchange Trading Hall Derivatives – via HKATS	No

Source – DMS Ltd

new markets and new regulations. Retail markets were not to be left out and so today we have fund supermarkets, closures of bank branches as customers 'preferred' online banking (not that the customers were asked or had any say in this), the demise of the insurance salesman, replaced by online information through computers, digital television and help desks, and the ability to take out a loan when you check out at your local supermarket.

So the shaping of today's marketplace has been a relatively recent event and yet even today the process of change continues. Behind the scenes settlement conventions (the number of days from the trade day that a transaction should settle on, i.e. T + 3) are shortening with the ultimate aim being to settle on trade day. The United States, Canada and Japan have all announced a desire to move to T + 1 from 2005, as the reduction in time from trade to settlement reduces the risk of a failure by one party to a trade. Yet the reduction in February 2001 from T + 5 to T + 3 in the UK had taken some 10 years to complete from the time that the G30, a private sector group that reviews the workings of the financial markets with a view to making recommendations on changes to improve efficiency and control risk in the markets, made it as one of their recommendations later taken up by the International Securities Services Association (ISSA) who have monitored these recommendations and since added to them. (See Appendix 2.)

Although it is of little interest to people buying their shares through an internet broker on their supermarket credit card, it is important for managers and supervisors to understand the issues involved in clearing and settling trades on different markets and in different products, as not only is it a fundamental part of the process but it also impacts in other ways, in particular on the way in which market participants work. For instance, market-makers will potentially sell stock they do not own, go short, and yet have to settle the trade perhaps only 3 days later. They can only trade in this way if they have a means to actually settle the trade, and so the ability to borrow stock from someone willing to lend it is crucial. A country or market that prohibits stock lending is potentially risking lack of liquidity because people cannot go short. In such a case buyers are forced to wait until there is a seller of stock or pay higher prices.

Liquidity is also affected where potential investors perceive that there are settlement problems in a market. This is sometimes the case with emerging markets where the opportunities to invest are potentially going to bring excellent returns and yet any gains may be quickly lost in administrative and settlement costs due to problems and delays.

Capital markets today are vibrant and offer fund-raising and investment opportunities to suit all. Sophisticated tailored products for international financing sit happily alongside more mundane premium savings bonds and unit trusts. The £5 a week paid into a life insurance policy may not seem very significant alongside the billions of pounds, dollars or euros changing hands daily in the markets. Yet in its own way that £5 is crucial because it is pooled with all the other £5's by the insurance company who can then invest what is now millions of pounds in shares and bonds and other instruments to provide the billions needed by those raising funds like governments, domestic and international corporate businesses and banks. Statistics do not always tell the true story but Figures 1.2–1.4 illustrate the changes in volumes of business or market capitalization of some of the major stock and derivatives markets, growth that could not have happened without radical changes in both trading and settlement.

	Value (£m)	No. of bargains
1997	1 012 534.70	13 346 346.00
1998	1 037 136.60	16 277 103.00
1999	1 410 590.00	21 076 558.00
2000	1 895 533.80	29 427 308.00
2001	**1 904 844.50**	**32 130 988.00**

Source: Business Analysis London Stock Exchange

Figure 1.2 UK equity turnover 1997–2001

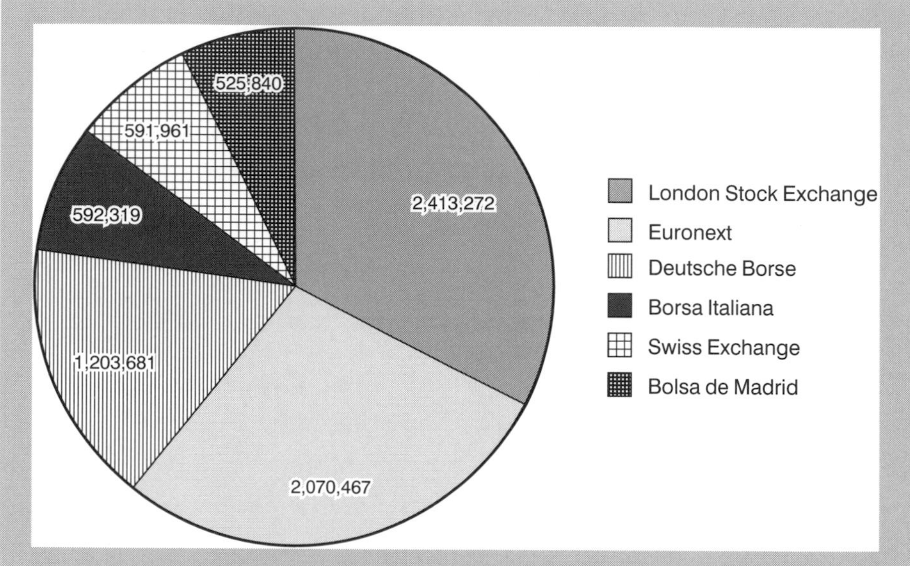

Figure 1.3 Market capitalizations at 31 December 2001 (€billion). (Source: *Next facts No. 7*, Euronext)

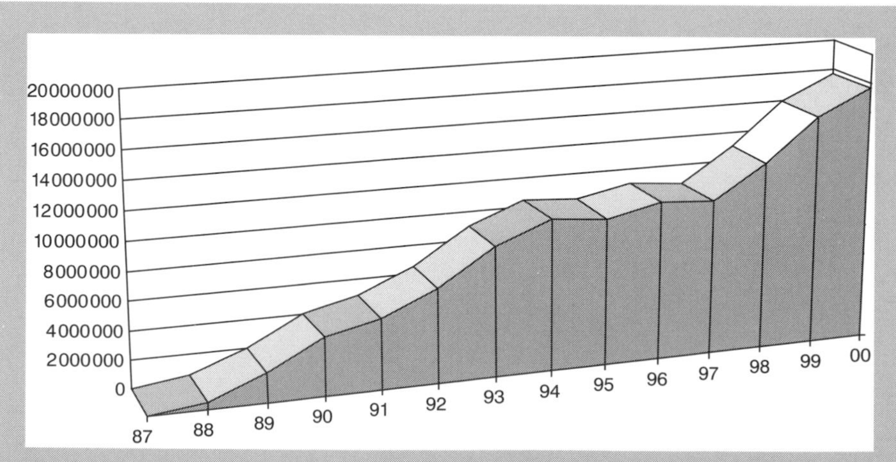

Figure 1.4 IPE Brent crude futures volumes, 1998–2000. (Source: *Pipeline magazine*, Issue 33, February 2002, International Petroleum Exchange)

It will be of no surprise, then, to learn that if change in the markets has been widespread and driven by technology, change in the operations function that supports the transactions has been just as widespread and significant. Technology has again been the main driver as the need to speed up the clearing and settlement process as well as increasing capacity in the firms became crucially important. Dematerialization, the paperless settlement of trades which utilizes electronic book entry recording of who owns the shares and the introduction of electronic trade confirmation systems and the development of the SWIFT[1] electronic messaging system were radical changes from the paper-intensive manual processes previously employed. But the growth in business and particularly international business also required more sophisticated systems to handle diverse products, different currencies, overseas resident clients and different regulatory environments. Today risk management is a key operations function, as is managing the use of collateral, added-value client services and regulatory compliance. Trade processing is still part of the operations role but in many organizations this is heavily automated as various stages of straight-through processing (STP) projects are completed and implemented.

No matter how large or small a transaction in the capital markets is, somewhere and at some time it must be cleared and settled and that is the role of operations. Naturally, operations teams need to understand how markets work and what clearing and settlement and indeed safekeeping requirements there will be for each market and product their organization and the clients of the organization deal in. No small task.

[1] The Society for Worldwide Interbank Financial Telecommunications.

Chapter 2

Debt and money markets

No small task. Indeed not, and consider Figure 2.1 that illustrates the UK's financial market structure as shown in the excellent *ISSA Handbook*.

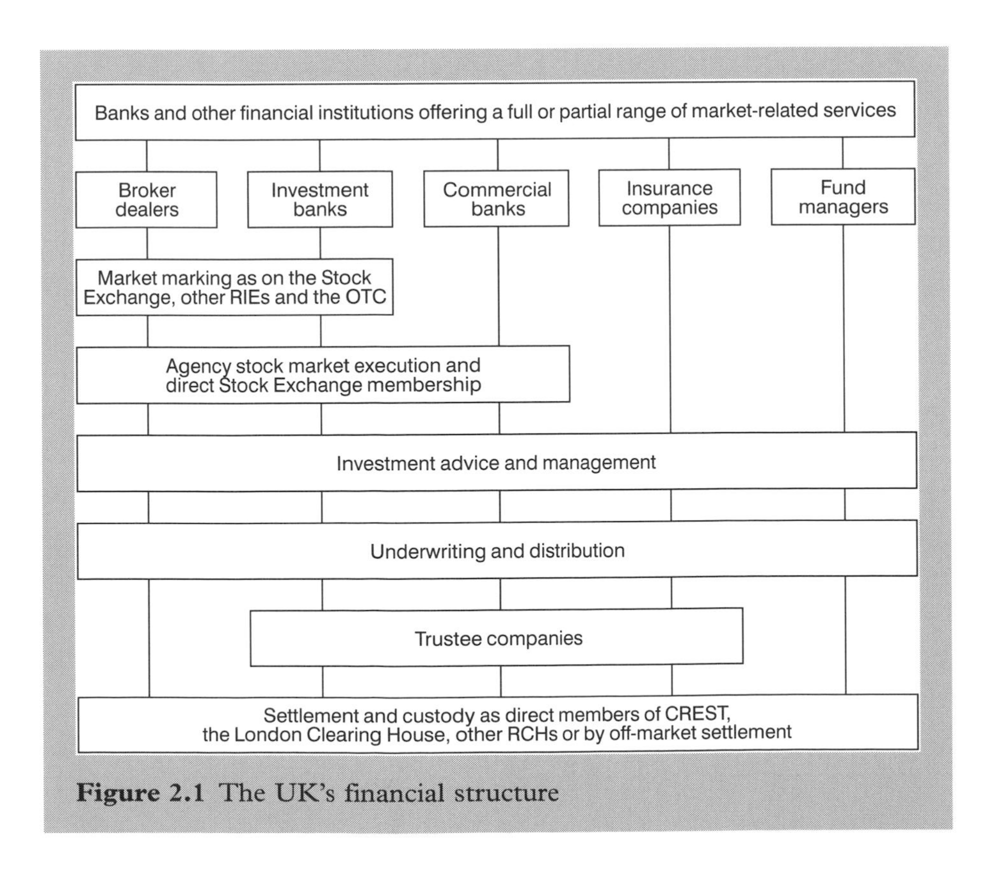

Figure 2.1 The UK's financial structure

If we assume therefore that the financial markets are structured into types or categories we can begin to look at the fundamental differences associated with each, explore the characteristics of the markets themselves and the products, which will determine the way in which the operations teams deal with them.

The wholesale and retail markets have different products, processes, procedures and participants. Often the retail market utilizes a combination of wholesale market products so that, for instance, a guaranteed equity index bond offered to the public will utilize the corporate bond market to give the financial return to allow the investors' subscriptions to be returned, and the derivatives market for the option contract on the index to guarantee the increase in the index value. We look at retail markets and products in more detail later in the book. The wholesale markets and distribution businesses of banks are constantly providing and utilizing products to satisfy the needs of financial management and capital generation for corporate clients and investment opportunities for institutions and private clients.

Corporate finance teams provide services to ensure that a client can raise funds to finance trading, research and development and use capital to acquire other businesses as well as defend a client against the predatory instincts of someone else. It is an often-complex process requiring great skill in relationship management, confidentiality, and a broad base of contacts. Raising millions of euros, dollars or pounds may sound easy but the instrument used to achieve this must be beneficial to both the client and the investor. Most importantly, it must be competitive with other types of investment opportunities and attractive. Thus we have different markets within the financial markets, all competing for an investor's money as they provide the capital sources that keep industry, commerce and governments working.

Taking debt and money markets first, we can safely assume that here we have products which are clearly defined, i.e. they represent a debt.

However, within this category are various types of debt instruments ranging from simple debt to a debt with conditions attached to it. In all cases an organization is borrowing money for a period of time. In the case of 'debt markets' this is usually for a period longer than 12 months. If a debt is for a shorter period of time it is often referred to as a money market instrument.

So we have common debt instruments like *bonds (*or *loan stocks), bills* and *notes*, for instance. A bond is issued by a borrower to a lender and in its simplest form is set for a period of time and carries a fixed rate of interest, payable at set times during the life of the bond. Then we have redemption, the return of the principal amount (the amount lent) and interest payments at periodic intervals, i.e. semi-annually or annually. In common with all financial markets there is a language

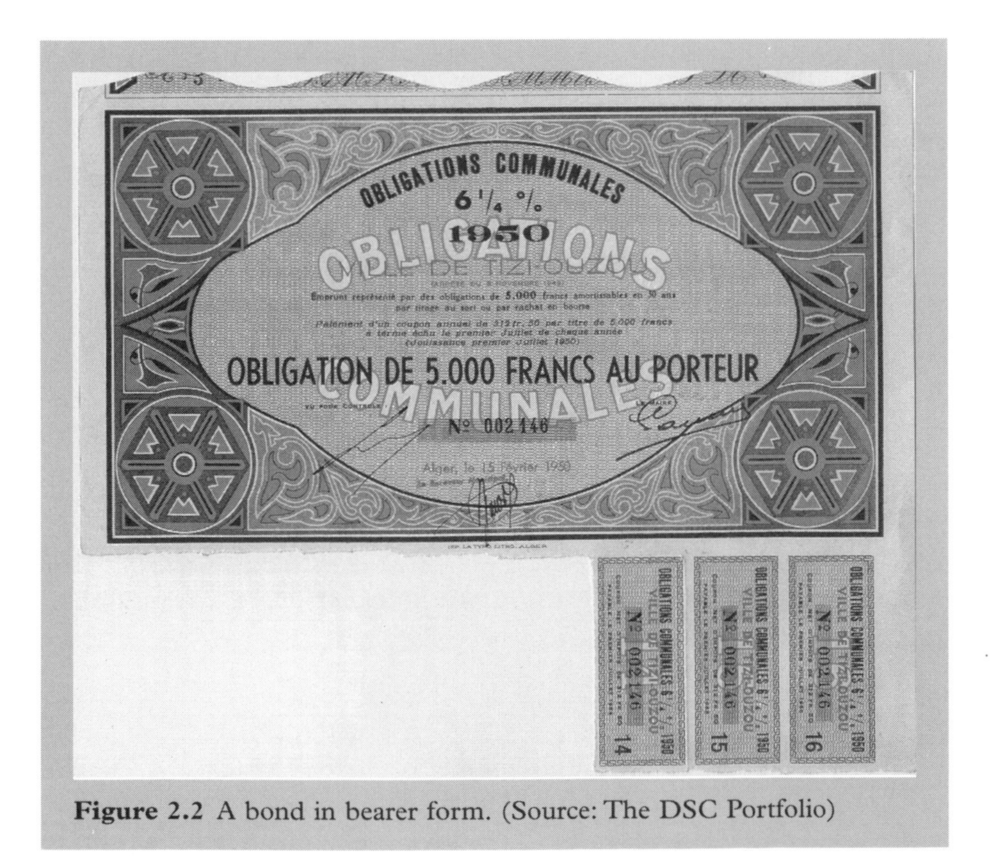

Figure 2.2 A bond in bearer form. (Source: The DSC Portfolio)

that is used and it is important that this language or terminology is understood or problems will undoubtedly occur. So when we talk about interest on a bond we could also refer to the *coupon* of the bond. Why? Well, bonds are often in bearer form and like a £10 banknote or a $1 bill whoever bears or has it in their hand owns it. If a bond is in bearer form (Figure 2.2) then the borrower has no means of knowing to whom the interest should be paid unless there is a facility, in this case a coupon attached to the bond, that can be detached, presented at the appropriate time to the paying agent of the borrower and the interest amount received in exchange.

The alternative to a bearer instrument is a registered instrument where a central register is kept of the owners of the instrument or security. The issuer of a registered security always knows who owns the debt but if the holder sells it, then the register must be updated to reflect the change in ownership. Typically bonds will be issued with a life or duration of anything from 3 years to 30 years or more and, unsurprisingly, are referred to as 'short', 'medium' and 'long' bonds.

In operations terms the issues are about:

- The type of bond, i.e. bearer or registered
- The frequency of the interest payments
- The rate of interest
- The date of redemption or duration of the bond

Additional information will include the paying agent, method of claiming interest and redemption amounts and whether there is any other condition, option or action that might occur with the bond on or before maturity.

Bonds with a predetermined rate of interest are known as fixed-rate or fixed-interest bonds. But bonds may also be issued with a floating or changeable rate of interest and these can be called *floating-rate notes* or FRNs. The precise terms of the interest, redemption and any other condition are decided when the instrument is issued, but exactly what the actual amounts or actions are will be determined at the appropriate times. We can illustrate this in Figure 2.3.

As well as fixed- and floating-rate bonds, investors may be tempted by bonds which have other characteristics. A *convertible bond* allows the holder to decide to convert or the issuer to convert the debt into, for instance, equity, i.e. shares in the company upon redemption.

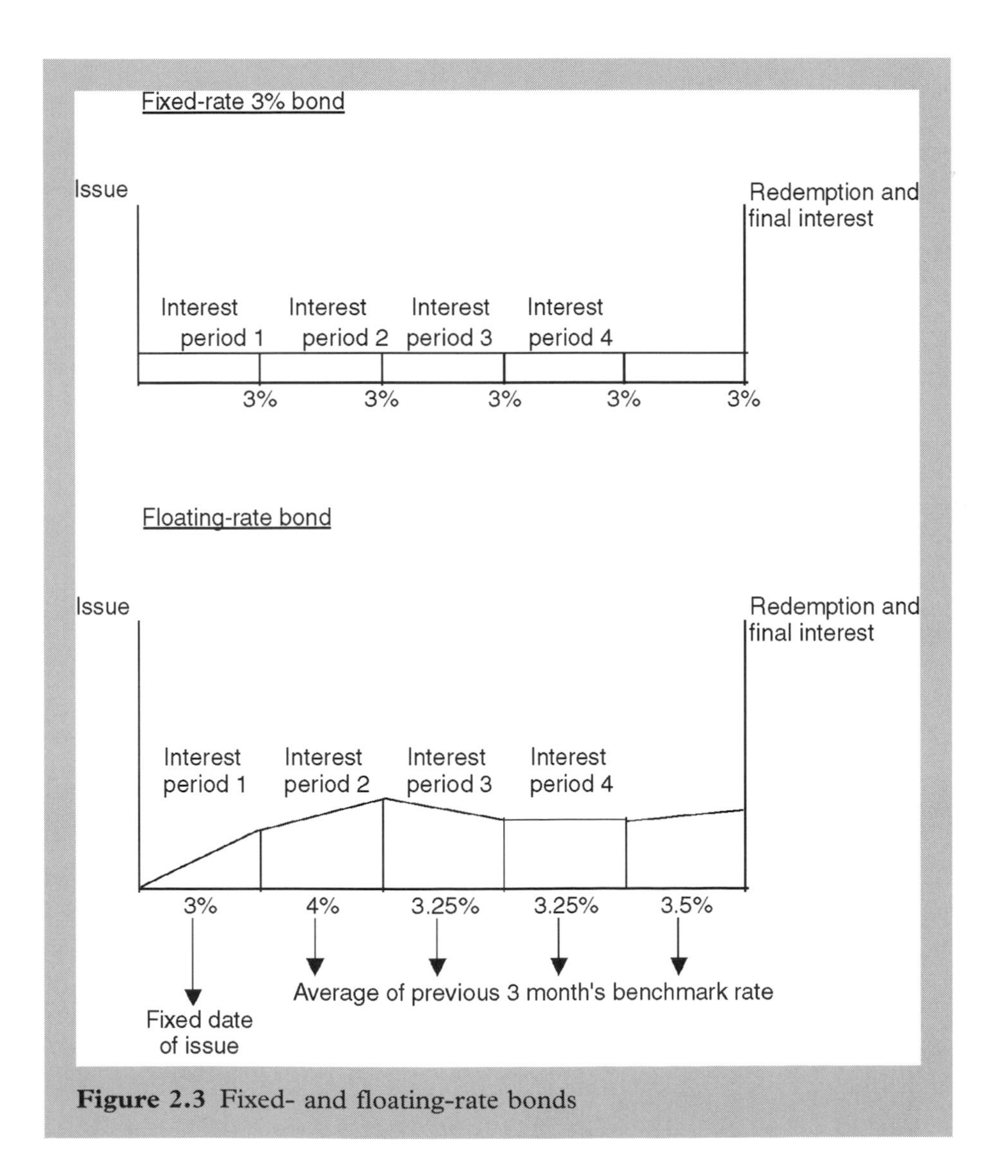

Figure 2.3 Fixed- and floating-rate bonds

Then we have *zero-coupon bonds* where instead of an interest amount being paid at intervals the bond is issued at a discounted price and then redeemed at the full face value (called at par), i.e. a bond with a face value of say £1000 is issued at £800. No interest is paid and when the bond reaches maturity the holder receives £1000. A fixed-income bond with a face value of £1000 is issued at £1000 and then interest is paid periodically until maturity, when the bond is redeemed for £1000.

Indexed bonds are popular as the interest rate is set at, say, 2% and is then 'topped up' if the rate of inflation or some other benchmark is higher so that the investor is guaranteed a return on their money of at least the inflation rate.

Bonds issued in the country of origin of the issuer are called domestic bonds, those by an international issuer in the currency of a country where they are issued are called a foreign bond. Those issued in a different country or countries from that in which the issuer is domiciled and in a different currency to where the issue takes place are called 'Eurobonds' or, more likely today, International bonds.

Governments or corporate entities issue bonds and the 'quality' of the issue is determined by the credit rating of the issuer. To some extent this can be seen in the interest rate paid by the borrower. Thus the bonds issued by, for instance, the UK government are called 'gilt-edged' or 'gilts', reflecting the almost 100% certainty that the debt and interest will be honoured. Contrast this with an emerging market government or a corporate seeking to borrow money where there is a greater chance that the debt or interest might not be honoured. The interest rate the UK government has to pay the lender will probably be lower than that of an emerging market or corporate.

If a debt or interest payment is not honoured, then a default has occurred. A default is usually a very serious issue for both the borrower and lender, resulting in claims for losses, reduction of credit-rating and ultimately the inability of the defaulting entity to borrow money and, in the case of a corporate, remain in business.

Credit ratings can also be affected by the performance of a country's economy or the corporate entity. An example of this is the downgrading of some airline stocks in the aftermath of the 11 September 2001 atrocities in the USA and increased competition from no-frills airlines which affected, for example, BA's profitability. Why was the downgrading important? Well, many investing institutions are permitted to hold 'paper', bonds, equities, etc. only of governments or companies with a certain credit rating or higher. If the credit rating falls below this minimum level the institution is forced to sell their holdings. At the same time, if the government or company is trying to raise additional finance, as it may well be, then the institutions cannot invest in that paper and it becomes harder and more expensive for the organization to raise money. As the interest rate is increased, to try to make it attractive to investors, so the yield or return becomes higher but the risk of default makes it a risky prospect. High-yield or junk bonds usually become an investment for only those with a high-risk appetite.

Most bonds have a fixed maturity date, when redemption of the bond takes place. However, some bonds carry conditions whereby the bond can be redeemed early or over a period of time. Examples are 'callable' and 'puttable' bonds, the former being where the issuer can seek to redeem the bond early, the latter the holder of the bond electing to redeem early. In both cases it may be a mandatory action or an option and full details of the terms for early redemption are set out when the bond is first issued. When early redemption takes place for a bearer stock, the issuer publishes details in the financial press and over news services indicating timetable, amounts and possibly the bond numbers. In some exceptional circumstances a bond is issued with no fixed maturity date and these are referred to as 'perpetual' bonds.

Money-market instruments include Treasury Bills and Notes as well as Certificates of Deposit. They are issued at a discount or with fixed or floating rates of interest.

Debt instruments are different in their structure and characteristics but in each case they are issued by a borrower and bought by an investor. The variety of maturities, rates and source of the issue provide investors with choices to suit their risk appetite, investment objectives and funds to invest. For instance, the private investor will often hold gilts but would be unlikely to participate in an International or Eurobond issue. Why? Well, it comes back to credit issues and in the case of an International bond the issue would be syndicated and placed with high credit-rated institutional clients rather than being offered to the public, whereas, in contrast, gilts can be purchased over the counter at a post office.

A key issue for dealers and fund managers in debt instruments is not what the price of the instrument is but rather what the yield is. After it is issued the price of a bond is dependent on interest rates. A bond issued with a fixed rate of 5% at a nominal or par value of £100 will not be priced at £100 if interest rates rise to 7%, quite simply because the yield or return is better at £7 on the 7% bond, so why pay the same money for the return of £5? Bond prices move in relation to interest rates so the price of the 5% bond will fall as the rates rise to 7% so that the yield on the 5% bond is near that of the current interest rate.

Calculating the actual yield on a bond is complicated and while it may be interesting to be able to know how the yield is calculated, for the operations team the yield on a bond is not the important information – the coupon or interest rate is. Irrespective of the yield the coupon will be paid based on the fixed or floating rate attributable to the particular bond.

What is particularly important is that bonds are traded with accrued interest, the amount of interest accumulated since the last payment.

Thus if we buy a bond today and it is half-way between interest payments we must pay the seller the interest accrued to date because we will receive the interest for the whole period since the last payment at the next payment date. Obviously if we were to sell the bond before the next payment we would receive the accrued interest up to the point at which we sold the bond.

Two issues, then, are (1) accurate static data in the systems on the instruments is crucial, and (2), procedures must be in place to ensure that any actions or events are managed. Conventions, i.e. settlement dates, frequency of coupon payments, etc. for debt and money market instruments vary across products and countries.

Operationally, however, there are fundamentally two prerequisites. First, if we are a buyer do we have the cash and, second, if we are a seller do we have the asset? Settlement problems will exist if these two fundamental settlement issues are not managed. In the market context, then, we need in operations to be aware of the liquidity of the assets in which we are dealing. If this is associated with another market, i.e. the bond is deliverable against a derivative position, the issue of liquidity becomes even greater. The benchmark bond in a market is generally the most liquid but this does not mean that the bonds themselves are liquid. Let us look at this more closely.

Government bond issues are usually fairly large so why would liquidity become an issue? The problem stems from the characteristic of the instrument. It is the type of investment product that will typically be held through to maturity. Large funds, pension funds, etc. will potentially hold large tranches of bonds. They know the return on the bond and the maturity so they can manage future cash flows in terms of pension payments quite effectively. Even changes in interest rates, and therefore yield, can be managed by using derivatives rather than trading the bonds. This means that although the issue is large, the amount of bonds actually changing hands during the life of the bond may be significantly smaller.

Instances where liquidity problems have surfaced include on the German derivatives exchange, EUREX. The number of futures contracts on the market that were open as expiry of the contract approached was so large that the market and the authorities were concerned that there would not be sufficient bonds available to meet the delivery obligations of the sellers of the futures contracts. As the participants in the bond and derivatives markets became aware of this the prices of the bonds that could be delivered rose sharply. A classic squeeze developed as many of the sellers of futures, therefore the holders of short positions, were faced with either paying a high price to buy the bonds and fulfil delivery of the future or a high price to buy back the futures position. In such a situation the losses could be substantial and so the authorities, i.e. the exchange, regulators and perhaps even government, will need to act to smooth the process through either setting financial requirements that force total speculators to close out their positions or to influence the price of the bond by issuing or releasing more bonds directly or indirectly into the market.

While we are on the subject of speculation and influences on markets we can look at foreign exchange. The currency markets of the world are significantly dominated by two factors, the perceived strength of the economy and therefore the actual use of the currency in commercial activity or to hedge against currency movements and the currency speculators. In today's global markets the speculators can move into and out of any asset very rapidly. They can also take or reduce exposures by operating in derivative products. They can, in some cases, operate on such a large scale that they can significantly move the price up or down. Who is this powerful? Well, some hedge funds for one, but more importantly not a single fund or organization but more a collective effort by several funds or organizations. Hence we have terms like 'a run on the currency'.

In most money market activity the central bank of a country is directly or indirectly involved. It has responsibilities to the government to ensure orderly markets take place and to protect the currency in line with government and bank policy, which will, of course, include managing inflation, credit, etc. When the twin forces of speculators and central banks go head-to-head it becomes a titanic struggle to gain the upper hand, and, as we saw in the UK, it is not always the bank that wins.

Faced with concerted selling of sterling prompted in part by the comments of a major hedge fund operator, George Soros, the government, through the Bank of England, decided to intervene in the markets and buy sterling to support the currency. This was important at the time, as sterling was part of the exchange rate mechanism for the future Euro currency. Several billion pounds were spent desperately trying to stop sterling crashing, and ultimately having to pull out of the exchange rate mechanism, all to no avail. The Bank of England could not stem the relentless selling of Soros and other hedge funds and speculators. Black Wednesday, as it was called, would cost the Chancellor of the Exchequer his job, and probably contributed to the downfall of the Conservative government, as the previously held opinion that the Conservatives were the best party to manage the economy was called into question.

The power of speculators in currencies is very real. It can affect most currencies at any time and while not always a disaster, authorities are always wary and the real markets (actual users of the currencies) will often hedge against the risk of a sudden adverse movement in the exchange rate against them. To do this they will often use products like derivatives, which we look at later in the book.

Operationally there is a need to be aware of both exchange rate movements and interest rate movements, which are often linked. FOREX deals will settle spot or forward. Spot is usually within two business days, forward is any agreed time, i.e. one week, one month, three months. In a global, multi-currency settlement environment it is imperative to ensure that exposures to currencies and interest rates are effectively managed. We talked earlier about liquidity being an issue in terms of assets being available and the funding of settlements, margin calls, etc. If we are faced with borrowing or, for that matter, taking off deposit a large amount of a currency to fund a settlement that subsequently does not take place when expected, we will get a lower rate, or conceivably no rate, on that cash overnight.

Money and the value of money is an important concept and many people in operations teams are not always aware of the value of money. The introduction of the euro helped to raise awareness of the value of money as the twelve participating countries fixed the rate of their existing currencies for conversion into the euro at midnight on 31 December 2001. Operationally at least, the result was a more simplified settlement process as twelve currencies became one. Balances in Deutsche marks, Francs and Lire were already, in many organizations, shown as the equivalent euros based on the conversion rates agreed, so 31 December 2001 became the date when notes and coins were changed, affecting the man and woman in the street and the retail banks more than other financial institutions.

Coming back to bonds, we have been talking about how bond dealers look at yields. Yields vary from instrument to instrument and, of course, very much so in the money markets. Cash deposited overnight will not attract the same level of interest rate as money borrowed or deposited for 3 months. Trying to predict future interest rates becomes part of dealing and investment decision. Dealers will look at creating yield curves to illustrate their expectations of rates over a period of time. Against the curve they will buy and sell and price instruments. Yield curves change as a result of actual rate changes and also the views of analysts. These views take into account the projected yield showing in different markets so that we might have short-term rates based on what the futures markets are saying and long-term rates based on the yield of the long bond.

What is the money value issue for operations teams? Inefficient use of cash, whether deposited or borrowed, can, depending on the size of the organization, have a profound effect on the cost of business and reduce the profit, or increase the loss, of the actual trade itself.

Treasury operations teams in banks and larger organizations will need to manage incoming and outgoing funds across several business areas and in several currencies. Failure to receive expected funds has an obvious impact on this process. So will leaving excess funds in a currency where the exchange rate has changed adversely or where the interest on the balance would be lower than if it were deposited elsewhere. The situation is compounded somewhat by the various services that are routinely offered by organizations to clients. Single-currency settlement is perhaps an obvious example and this is looked at further in another book in this series. Essentially the receipt of a currency to be held against obligations generated in another currency is the taking of an exchange rate exposure offset by the convenience to the client (and counterpart) in administration. Failure to monitor and manage the exposure could result in a currency loss when the profit/loss is finally realized in the underlying currency.

Fund managers in multi-currency investments are aware of this exchange rate risk and often undertake a hedging transaction at the time of the investment so that there is no sudden change to the published performance of the fund. The term used is a 'currency overlay'.

We began this chapter by looking at the characteristics of bonds and talked about coupons and redemptions. Now we can see the impact of this in the Treasury processes, as coupon payments and redemptions are included into the cash forecasting, based on the expected settlement date according to the conventions of the market, product and country concerned.

The bond and money markets are huge. Statistics can sometimes be misleading and at other times of little value. So when we say the bond market in a particular country is *X* billion dollars or *Y* billion euros is it significant? Well, the answer with bonds is yes because we are talking about debts. If the government bond market is of a significant size then the country is heavily in debt and likewise when we talk about corporate bonds. If a company has a significant amount of bonds in issue it has a large debt to pay off and, of course, will often have to find the capital to pay the interest on that debt for many years. The size of debt markets is a pointer to the wellbeing or otherwise of the entity or economy concerned. So is debt bad? Not necessarily. A government may choose to borrow money rather than keep raising and lowering taxes, its other source of finance. In the UK this is called the Public Sector Net Cash Requirement (PSNCR). However, if tax receipts are high, perhaps because of good growth and financial stability which generates higher profits for businesses and therefore higher corporation tax payments, the government is unlikely to issue further debt and may choose to reduce the debt in issue by redeeming existing bonds.

Companies may want to raise cash through bonds rather than issuing shares or borrowing money at a bank for various reasons. This will include the cost of the borrowing. Money has value and the cost of financing debt will have a significant, possibly devastating, effect on a company. Enron, an energy company in the USA is a prime example of this. It went into liquidation in early 2002 as the largest ever collapse of a corporate business with massive debts and, allegedly unrecognized losses. The sheer cost of paying the debt bankrupted the company and also created untold problems for other companies that had lent it money.

In many respects we can draw a similar picture in banking and investment management. The policy behind trading and investment is not simply about making a profit, but is also about the most effective way to achieve the end result. That may mean funding a position or purchase for a period of time. The cost of the funding is taken into account in the strategy decision and, when appropriate, in the price of purchase as well as any resale. The final profit or loss is therefore the combination of the traded prices and the cost of the finance.

From an operations point of view we need to think about issues like reporting the cost of funding positions, settlement, income from the bonds, etc. This will be important to the final profit/loss calculation. We will also need to consider the source of prices for valuation purposes and this may be a problem if we are operating in illiquid bonds, as some corporate bonds may well be. We also need to assess the value of bonds in terms of collateral use and again liquidity will be an issue. If there is a shortage of particular bonds we hold then there may be excellent opportunities to utilize those bonds in stock lending. Likewise, if we need to borrow bonds what other bonds might we offer as collateral? We come back to credit rating and valuations.

A change in interest rates is of great significance operationally as it will change the value of bonds as yields change, affecting collateral, volumes, liquidity, etc. It will prompt changes in floating-rate notes, alter the yield or return on deposits, require rates to be changed on systems and for any deposits held on behalf of clients. In some cases it may prompt an action like the early redemption of a bond or affect the merits of converting the bond for a share or different bond. Of course, with a convertible bond any change in the price of the underlying equity stock will also be important and, as this can be affected by what happens with exchange rates, careful monitoring is essential, particularly if conversion is imminent.

As funding costs and returns change we must also be aware of fluctuations in an exchange rate against different currencies, prompting further adjustments and altering the dealing strategies, which in turn generate new inflows and outflows.

Naturally the above comments about data, procedures, cash and assets are also true of equity, commodity and derivatives markets. Do we need therefore to establish any other factors about debt and money markets before we look at equities, derivatives and commodities?

Given that the volume of business being processed is one of the core operations functions, what else, other than interest rate or exchange movements, can affect the bond and money markets and therefore the operations teams?

In essence we have already answered that. There are various events that can occur either as a mandatory action or as a voluntary action. Redemption of a bond may be variable or fixed while most money-market instruments have a fixed redemption.

Bond and money markets are obviously technical markets and the reader should be aware that we have not even begun to scratch the surface of the intricacies of bond pricing, duration management, etc. However, we have looked at the important characteristics from an operations point of view.

Bonds and money-market settlement teams need, as all settlement teams do, good working relationships with the dealing side and clients if the process is to be managed successfully. Timing of information, actions and deadlines is always important but with most government bonds and money market instruments settling T + 1 to T + 3 and corporate bonds T + 3 there is little room for error in the bond trading and settlement cycle.

Chapter 3

Equity markets

Equity markets are diverse. There are the exchanges which deal with listed shares of the largest companies in the world and exchanges, sometimes the same ones, dealing with fledgling companies. There are also unlisted securities.

Equity markets are high profile. The news bulletins on television and radio often refer to the rise or fall of the local index on the stock market. Many private investors start their portfolios with equity shares, sometimes from incentive schemes operated by their employers or as a result of a government privatizing a hitherto-nationalized industry. The policy of the Conservative government in the UK, under Margaret Thatcher, created thousands of new investors with the selling off of companies and utilities like British Telecom and British Gas. Share options are a popular way to reward and 'lock-in' employees, as this option gives them the opportunity to convert to shares and have a stake in the company and thus its success.

Equity markets therefore act as another kind of barometer of the wellbeing of a country, reflecting the prospects of manufacturing, services, utilities, etc. They also offer good value to the investor as both a profit, as a result of an increase in share price, and a return, in the form of dividends, is possible. Possible is the key word here. Unlike most debt, which will result in the par value being redeemed and some debt where the return in the form of interest is fixed, equity is totally different. An investor might buy shares and never receive a dividend and see the company go into liquidation, making the shares worthless.

To raise capital companies can, as an alternative to issuing debt, issue equity in the form of ordinary shares in the UK, common stock in the USA and similar titles in other countries. Unlike debt and money-market instruments, however, the issuing of shares will, in most cases, give away part-ownership of the business. Shareholders have rights, including the right to vote on issues presented as resolutions at an annual general meeting (AGM) which the company must call each year. Information must be made available to shareholders and this includes the remuneration of the directors of the company and any information that might have a material impact on the price of the shares. The rights of shareholders in the UK are governed by company law, while the rules covering listing on a stock exchange, disclosure of information, etc. are under the control of the regulator, the Financial Services Authority (FSA).

There are different classes of equity that can be issued by a company. Ordinary shares may have conditions attached so that they can be issued as voting or non-voting shares. In some cases separate classes of shares are issued for domestic and foreign investors. There are also preference shares, where the dividend is paid to the holder of these securities before the ordinary shareholders. In the UK ordinary shares have a nominal value, for example *ordinary 50p shares*, a value that must be paid for them to be called fully paid shares and thereby able to participate fully in dividend and other distributions, voting etc.

Equity shares differ from debt instruments in several key ways as Table 3.1 shows.

For the operations teams the main issues are the settlement conventions and the impact of market conditions on the underlying shares, in particular those that lead to different types of corporate

Table 3.1 The differences between equity shares and debt instruments

Equity shares	Debt instruments
Ordinary, preference shares	Bonds, loan stock
Part-ownership of company, has rights like voting	Loan to company
Usually registered securities	Often bearer securities
Income paid in dividend (ordinary shares)	Income paid in interest (called coupon)
Income paid in interest (preference shares)	Zero coupon instruments issued at a discount, no interest
Duration: until the company ceases to exist through take-over, merger or liquidation or if the shares are bought back by the company	Duration: usually a fixed redemption date or date(s), can be continuous (called perpetual)

Source: DMS Ltd.

actions or events where a benefit is distributed to the shareholder, a take-over, merger, de-merger or similar event occurs. In both cases the situation varies depending on the market's geographical location, whether the equity products are traded heavily by international investors, the degree of regulation in the market and the extent to which electronic trading dematerialized settlement exists. We must also be aware that there are many equity products apart from shares. We have indices, exchange traded funds (ETFs), equity derivatives, basket trades and numerous retail products based on equities.

The trading of equities varies from straight transactions in shares or derivatives to sometimes complex combinations of deals, such as simultaneous trading in shares and derivatives or transactions in the shares of many different companies as a single deal, hence the term *basket* or sometimes *program* trade. Equity products are also sector based so that we have, for instance, the 'oil sector', and these sectors often generate indices and subsequently several products based on those indices or sectors. In the retail markets there are products based not only on equities but on a geographical grouping of equities, for example 'European Funds', Asia-Pacific Funds', etc. To facilitate diversity, sector coverage, efficient investment and benchmarking, many indices have been developed. Traders and investors either deal directly in shares included in the indices or in products based on the indices, and will often benchmark the return on their investments based on the performance of their portfolio in comparison to the rise or fall in the value of the relevant index or indices.

Major equity markets around the world have at least one index and often several indices. An example would be the **FTSE Family** and the **Euronext 100 index** the composition of which is shown in Figure 3.1.

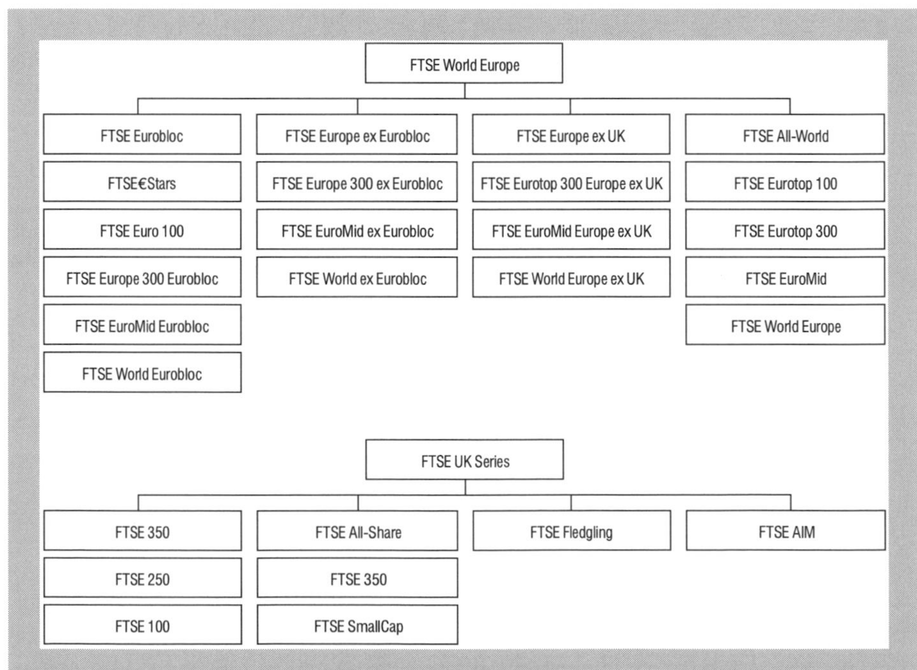

Figure 3.1 The European Index family tree. (Source: *FTSE Monthly Review*)

DJ Euro STOXX 50 Option
DJ Euro STOXX 50 Future
DJ Euro STOXX Banks Option
DJ Euro STOXX Banks Future
DJ Euro STOXX Healthcare Option
DJ Euro STOXX Healthcare Future
DJ Euro STOXX Technology Option
DJ Euro STOXX Technology Future
DJ Euro STOXX Telecom Option
DJ Euro STOXX Telecom Future
DJ STOXX 50 Option
DJ STOXX 50 Future
DJ STOXX 600 Banks Future
DJ STOXX 600 Healthcare Future
DJ STOXX 600 Technology Future
DJ STOXX 600 Telecom Future
Dow Jones Global Titans 50 Option
Dow Jones Global Titans 50 Future
DAX Option
DAX Future
NEMAX 50 Option
NEMAX 50 Future
SMI Option
SMI Future
HEX25 Option (OFOX)
HEX25 Future (FFOX)

Figure 3.2 Eurex Index products

To give an idea of the index products developed for a region we can look at those indices on which one of Europe's leading derivatives exchanges, EUREX, has based their products (Figure 3.2).

As another example the following are some examples of the leading US indices:[1]

[1] Information on the US indices was found from a variety of sources including www.bigcharts.marketwatch.com and www.raymondjames.com

- The Dow Jones Industrial Average is a price-weighted average of 30 blue-chip stocks, which are generally the leaders in their industry and are listed on the New York Stock Exchange. It has been a widely followed indicator of the stock market since 1 October 1928.
- The Dow Jones Transportation Average is a price-weighted average of 20 transportation stocks, which are listed on the New York Stock Exchange.
- The Dow Jones Utilities Average is a price-weighted average of 15 utility companies, which are listed on the New York Stock Exchange and who are involved in the production of electrical energy.
- The Dow Jones Composite Average is a price-weighted average of 65 stocks, which trade on the New York Stock Exchange. The average is a combination of the Dow Jones Industrial, Transportation and Utilities Averages.
- The Standard & Poor's 100 Index is a capitalization-weighted index based on 100 highly capitalized stocks for which options are listed on the CBOE.
- The Standard & Poor's 500 Index is a capitalization-weighted index of 500 stocks designed to measure performance of the broad domestic economy through changes in the aggregate market value of 500 stocks representing all major industries.
- The Standard & Poor's Midcap 400 is a capitalization-weighted index, which measures the performance of the mid-range sector of the US stock market.
- The Standard & Poor's Smallcap 600 Index is a capitalization-weighted index, which measures the performance of selected US stocks with a small market capitalization.
- The NYSE Composite Index is a capitalization-weighted index, which includes all companies listed on the New York Stock Exchange.
- The Philadelphia Value Line Index is a price-weighted index developed to track the performance of the overall US economy.
- The Wilshire 5000 Equity Index measures the performance of all US-headquartered equity securities with readily available price

data. The index is an excellent approximator of dollar changes in the US equity market.

- The NASDAQ Composite Index is a broad-based capitalization-weighted index of all NASDAQ National Market & SmallCap stocks.
- The NASDAQ-100 Index is a capitalization-weighted index of the 100 largest OTC stocks.
- The Russell 1000 Index measures the performance of the 1000 largest companies in the Russell 3000 Index, which represents approximately 90% of the total market capitalization of the Russell 3000 Index.
- The Russell 2000 Index is composed of the smallest 2000 companies in the Russell 3000 Index, representing approximately 11% of the Russell 3000 total market capitalization.
- The Russell 3000 Index measures the performance of the 3000 largest US companies based on total market capitalization, which represents approximately 98% of the investable US equity market.

Other important US indices include:

- American Stock Exchange Composite Index
- Fortune 500 Index
- 30-Year Treasury Bond Index
- CBOE Gold Index
- AMEX Major Market Index
- PSE Technology Index

The various indices of the markets worldwide are, as we have noted, used in a variety of ways and by various entities and investors. An index is created to be representative of the leading shares in a market. The Financial Times Stock Exchange 100 Index, better known as the FTSE 100 or the *'footsie'*, consists of the leading 100 shares listed on the London Stock Exchange ranked by capitalization and weighted to reflect each shares percentage of the overall index. The market capitalization is the number of shares in issue multiplied by the mid price of the shares, and thus the capitalization of companies changes particularly as the share price changes, and so too does that of the companies ranking within the index. The greater the capitalization and ranking the higher the weighting such that a significant movement in price of the hundredth ranked stock will have the same impact on the value of the index as a much smaller movement in the share price of the company ranked first in the index.

Turnover is high in the shares of companies in indices as they are used for so many investment and benchmarking purposes, as well as having many derivative products based on them. It is therefore important for operations teams to be aware of the shares in the various major indices and how volatile the share price is. They must also know which markets the shares are traded on, whether it is electronic or open-outcry trading, if they are traded over-the-counter as well as on exchanges, whether they are in registered or bearer form and settlement dematerialized, how easy it is to settle these shares and who the clearing house is, what the expected dividend announcement and pay dates are, who the company registrar or agent is, etc. This information is vital as trading, clearing and settlement processes may be straightforward, highly automated and dematerialized or complex, manual and certificated.

On 31 December 2001 the FTSE 100 consisted of the companies shown in Table 3.2, each of which is traded on the Stock Exchange Electronic Trading System (SETS), considered in greater detail in Chapter 5.

Today so much dealing and investment in equities is via index-based products that one would be forgiven for thinking that nobody trades the humble ordinary share. To some extent that is true. In the UK the percentage of private client transactions in equity shares has fallen and instead the investment tends to be made in retail products like unit trusts. There are several reasons for this: partially cost, partially the lack of awareness of the markets and also losses. Many small investors, having been tempted by the UK government's privatization

Table 3.2 The FTSE 100 on 31 December 2001

Rank	Security	Rank	Security
1	BP	52	Royal & Sun Alliance Insurance Group
2	GlaxoSmithKline	53	Imperial Tobacco Group
3	Vodafone Group	54	3i Group
4	HSBC Hldgs	55	Land Securities
5	Astrazeneca	56	Alliance & Leicester
6	Royal Bank of Scotland Group	57	Dixons Group
7	Shell Transport & Trading Co	58	Allied Domecq
8	Lloyds TSB Group	59	Amersham
9	Barclays	60	Invensys
10	HBOS	61	Shire Pharmaceuticals Group
11	Diageo	62	South African Breweries
12	BT Group	63	Smiths Group
13	CGNU	64	Scottish & Newcastle
14	Anglo American	65	Smith & Nephew
15	Unilever	66	Old Mutual
16	Tesco	67	Friends Provident
17	Abbey National	68	Man Group
18	Rio Tinto	69	Granada
19	Prudential	70	Hilton Group
20	Compass Group	71	Hanson
21	Marks & Spencer	72	Hays
22	BAE Systems	73	ARM Holdings
23	British American Tobacco	74	United Utilities
24	BG Group	75	Gallaher Group
25	Centrica	76	Safeway
26	BHP Billiton	77	Wolseley
27	Standard Chartered	78	Next
28	Cadbury Schweppes	79	Sage Group
29	Reuters Group	80	Morrison (Wm) Supermarkets
30	Legal & General Group	81	Enterprise Oil
31	WPP Group	82	Canary Wharf Group
32	Scottish Power	83	Northern Rock
33	Amvescap	84	Capita Group
34	Reed International	85	P & O Princess Cruises
35	Cable & Wireless	86	British Land Co
36	BAA	87	Rolls-Royce
37	National Grid Group	88	EMI Group
38	GUS	89	Severn Trent
39	mm02	90	Imperial Chemical Industries
40	Pearson	91	Logica
41	Reckitt Benckiser	92	Brambles Industries
42	British Sky Broadcasting Group	93	International Power
43	Six Continents	94	Innogy Hldgs
44	Boots Co	95	British Airways
45	Lattice Group	96	Electrocomponents
46	Sainsbury (J)	97	Schroders
47	Scottish & Southern Energy	0	Schroders N/V
48	Rentokil Initial	98	Celltech Group
49	Kingfisher	99	Associated British Foods
50	BOC Group	100	Daily Mail & General Trusts (A Shs)
51	Powergen		

Source: *FTSE European Monthly Review*, January 2002.

programme, were badly affected by the market crash of 1987, for instance. However, the privatization programme, introduction of Internet trading and the sustained growth in equity markets over several years saw a reversal of the trend.

The characteristics of equity shares make them more unpredictable or speculative than, say, fixed-income bonds. Whereas the bond will pay a known fixed amount of income and will be redeemed on maturity, the ordinary share offers no such guarantees. Income in the form of dividends will be dependent on profits. Capital gain in terms of an increase in the share price will be dependent on the performance of the company, its competitors and the whole market. The latter is, of course, governed by domestic and global considerations, the performance of the government in managing the economy, global growth or recession and in particular the performance of the US economy, as its vast consumption and production tends to affect businesses in all the markets of the world. The return on other types of products is also a factor, so if interest rates rise and investors switch money from buying shares to buying bonds, the equity market will likely fall.

So what determines the price of equities? Essentially the price of a share reflects the historical performance of the company and the expected performance. The annual report and accounts, a legal requirement, provides information on the past performance of the company, including the profit or loss for the current and previous periods of the report, the balance sheet and details of the assets the company holds. The directors also provide their report to shareholders on the performance, including the recommendation for the dividend payment, if any, and the expectations for the next year and beyond. Analysts at the banks, brokers and some institutional clients as well as the financial press will then look at the figures, facts and statements, compare them with the competition and with the expectations based on the previous report, build in their views on the domestic and global economy, the sector, etc. and finally produce their analysis and often their recommendation on whether to buy, hold or sell the shares.

The analysts' findings are often crucial in the decision-making process by fund managers and as a result there is considerable store placed on a broker that has the top-rated analysts for particular sectors. Fund managers will, of course, also receive presentations directly from companies, particularly if the company is wishing to raise money or change the capital structure by, for instance, having a rights issue or share split, and, of course, if there is any take-over or merger activity. In fact whenever the company is seeking shareholder support it needs to be very active in making its case to those shareholders.

Shares, like bonds, are first issued in the primary market and subsequently traded in the secondary market. In terms of the primary market, the company will seek a listing on a stock exchange, publish a prospectus setting out the aims and expectations of the business and the terms for subscribing for the shares and, if all goes well, will receive sufficient applications for the shares to raise the capital they need. Once completed the issued shares can then be traded on the exchange.

In reality it is not quite so simple. In most cases a company seeking a public listing will engage the specialist services of a bank or broker to ensure that all the regulatory issues are dealt with, that the price of the shares offered is neither too high nor too low given the capital requirements and the market conditions, and to seek underwriting of the issue so that if there is a problem in obtaining enough subscription from the public the underwriters will take up the shares and the company will receive its capital. It may be that the broker offers to place the shares with its institutional clients rather than have a public offering.

For operations teams the lead up to and the outcome of an initial public offering (IPO) will be important. First, there is the process of meeting the deadlines for the application(s), funding for the application arranged and then dealing with the subsequent allocation of the new shares. We will look at these three stages later, but the success or otherwise of the issue will depend on the market and the appetite of the investors for the shares.

An IPO is not guaranteed to be a success, despite the best efforts of the corporate finance teams advising the company. On the other hand, an IPO, such as the government privatization of British Telecommunications plc, was always going to be successful because of the attractive price and huge amount of advertising of the offer. The offer was also biased towards the small shareholder so that the investment funds would not receive the full amount they applied for. The BT float was duly oversubscribed. This oversubscription meant that the amounts applied for were scaled down and the balance of the monies returned to the applicant. As the BT offer was biased towards the small shareholder applications for a few hundred shares were likely to be fully met while the applications for several million shares would be only partially successful. What it did do was generate enormous interest and demand in the shares when they started trading in the secondary markets as the unsuccessful applicants tried to purchase additional shares for their portfolios. In some cases large and small applications may, in the case of an oversubscription, simply go into a ballot to be drawn until the offered amount is completed and will therefore be successful or unsuccessful. In some cases an IPO is cancelled when the market conditions make it unlikely to be successful and the cost of underwriting the offer is too prohibitive. The offer may be postponed or, if the company needs the capital urgently, some other source of raising the money will be sought.

The three stages for operations are initially, the application for the issue including the amount applied for, the payment required, completion of the document giving the name in which the shares will be registered, the name of any agent acting on our behalf, etc. and the depositing of the application with the company's agent before the deadline.

Secondly, it must be ensured that the correct amount for the shares applied for was included and has been incorporated into the firm's cash flow management as the company agent may pay in the subscription amounts prior to the allocation or otherwise of the shares and return any balance at a later date.

Finally, once the allocation of the shares offered has been published and notification received of the number allotted to the firm, the records need to be updated to reflect the initial position on the book or in the fund. The shares or security will be given a unique identifying number by the exchange that will be used in the matching and settlement process and this and other important data will be set up on the database for the systems.

In essence the same scenario applies for unlisted securities, except, of course, the listing element doesn't apply. Shares issued in small companies tend initially to be held by the owners, who are also the directors, and perhaps a few family and friends, but whether the shares are issued by small or large companies they must be part of the authorized share capital.

To raise capital companies issue shares. Rather than being a debt that has to be repaid they are the sale (by the company) and purchase (by the investor) of part-ownership of the company. The initial share price is the offer price in the primary market; thereafter the secondary market determines the price of the shares. The price of an equity is, as we have already noted, determined by several factors both historical and based on expectation. Just like with bonds and other instruments, liquidity is also an issue and so too is the return on the investment. The return on the bond is the yield represented by the interest paid during the life of the bond. With an equity the yield is based on the amount of dividend. The dividend yield is the amount of dividend distributed divided by the share price multiplied by 100.

A high-priced share is not necessarily more expensive than a cheaper share as, relatively speaking a company with a share price of, say, £3.50, a dividend yield of 3.5% and a P/E of 50 is more expensive

Example

If a company had a distributed dividend of 35p and a share price of 566p the dividend yield would be:

$35/566 \times 100 = 6.18\%$

So the dividend yield on this share is pretty good if, say, inflation is running at 2.5% but is the share price high or low? There is no easy answer to that but one measurement which could be looked at is the price/earnings ratio. Assume the company has profits of £5m and 15m shares in issue. Each share is earning 33p (5 million divided by 15 million) called the earnings per share (EPS) but what is the price/earnings or P/E ratio? The P/E can be found by dividing the share price by the EPS, e.g.

$566/33 = 17.15$

The share price is trading on a multiple of 17 times its earnings. Clearly the investors buying shares at that price believe the company will do well in the future and increase the earnings per share accordingly. However, if the company failed to meet expectations then the investors may become wary about the company's prospects, including its ability to maintain the dividend, and will start to sell the shares. A cut in the dividend paid by a company usually triggers a fall in the share price because it is a pointer to lower earnings per share, in other words lower profits. Conversely, a share might rise in price if the company announces a reduction in the workforce and cost savings if orders fall because the cost base is being reduced and the profit margin is hopefully being maintained on lower earnings.

than the shares of a company currently priced at £10 with a 6% dividend yield and a P/E of 20. Why? Because the yield is lower and the P/E higher on the company with the share price of £3.50 than the company with a share price of £10, suggesting that investors are paying a high price in expectation of the company doing well in the future compared to the other company with a higher dividend yield and much more earnings per share and hence lower P/E. The more cautious investor might buy the shares of the second company whereas the speculator might be prepared to gamble on the first company producing the results the share price is suggesting will occur.

The dotcom bubble burst when investors realized that many shares, which were trading on massive P/Es based on expectations for the future, would in reality be unlikely to deliver the results that justified such a high P/E. Consequently the shares seemed over-priced and as companies became unable to raise any more funding from backers and began to fail, the reality began to dawn and the panic buying that had driven the shares to crazy levels was replaced by panic selling. Investors realized that the so-called 'old economy' stocks which had modest P/Es were perhaps more robust and a better long-term investment than the 'new economy' stocks launched in the late 1900s and early 2000s many of which had disappeared by 2002.

Share price, naturally enough, affects the volume of business in equities, but so too do the requirements of the various investment, life and pension funds and, of course, the hedge funds. Their influence on the markets is significant at times whether they are buying or selling. So too is the performance of the economy, rising interest rates and poor exchange rates being considered bad news for equities, the latter particularly so for exporters if the currency is very strong, as this makes the products more expensive in overseas countries. The strength or otherwise of the equities markets is reflected in the amount of activity in areas such as mergers and acquisitions, capital raising and/or restructuring. When equity markets are strong, companies will be more inclined to expand by either take-overs and mergers or raising extra capital. This generates plenty of work for corporate finance teams and thus fee income for the banks. The activity also offers fund managers and investors opportunities to invest their money and this together with buoyant company profits and therefore good dividend yields attracts more investors to the equity markets.

This process can go on for many years and indeed did so through much of the 1990s and into the new millennium as the US economy was strong and other economies like those in the UK, Europe and Asia followed suit. Even problems with some emerging markets failed to dent the relentless rise until growth started to slow. At first markets stopped climbing ever higher and then as concerns grew over growth prospects in the US markets, global markets started to fall back. This can be illustrated by the fall in equity issues in the global markets from Q1 1996 to Q3 2001 shown in Table 3.3 with data obtained from the Bank for International Settlements.

As companies began to feel the pinch of slower economies, so the profits began to drop and this spilled over into lower dividend income and falling share prices, which reduced gains made over the previous years. Private investors and fund managers started to look at realizing some of these gains by selling their equities. With fewer buyers around, share prices were pushed lower and, coupled with predictions of inflationary pressures, interest rate rises and much slower growth, investors started looking at other ways to invest their money.

The impact on operations teams was to be profound as volumes of business dropped significantly. Many equity operations teams had themselves grown during the long period of growth in the equity markets, processing ever greater numbers of equity bargains, cash and foreign exchange transactions, dealing with the aftermath of many mergers, acquisitions and other corporate actions such as rights issues and capital restructuring. Fund managers developed and

Table 3.3 The fall in equity issues in the global markets, 1996–2001

Announced international equity issues by nationality of issuer (in billions of US dollars)	1996-Q1	1996-Q2	1996-Q3	1996-Q4	1997-Q1	1997-Q2	1997-Q3	1997-Q4
All countries	16.5	23.8	15.9	25.4	20.3	35.1	21.2	42.9
Developed countries	11.5	19.7	10.3	17.6	14.6	24.5	14.1	34.4
Offshore centres	2.3	1.1	2.0	2.1	1.9	1.7	1.0	1.1
Developing countries	2.7	3.0	3.6	5.8	3.8	8.9	6.1	7.4
Asia and Pacific	1.5	2.4	1.9	2.6	3.2	3.9	2.7	5.0
Europe	0.3	0.1	0.2	0.7	0.2	1.2	0.6	1.2
Latin America and Caribbean	0.3	0.3	1.2	1.6	0.1	1.9	1.8	1.1
	1998-Q1	**1998-Q2**	**1998-Q3**	**1998-Q4**	**1999-Q1**	**1999-Q2**	**1999-Q3**	**1999-Q4**
All countries	26.2	51.4	17.0	31.3	34.9	62.2	43.9	74.8
Developed countries	21.8	46.2	16.4	27.4	31.4	51.8	32.0	62.6
Offshore centres	1.5	1.3	0.1	0.9	1.1	3.6	3.7	4.7
Developing countries	2.9	3.8	0.5	2.9	2.5	6.8	8.2	7.6
Asia and Pacific	1.9	1.9	0.2	0.9	1.3	5.7	5.0	5.0
Europe	0.8	1.0	0.2	0.7	0.3	0.4	0.1	0.5
Latin America and Caribbean	–	0.2	0.1	–	0.2	–	0.3	0.3
	2000-Q1	**2000-Q2**	**2000-Q3**	**2000-Q4**	**2001-Q1**	**2001-Q2**	**2001-Q3**	
All countries	98.3	90.4	62.6	65.2	38.2	56.4	19.2	
Developed countries	81.8	74.7	48.4	51.7	34.2	50.5	17.6	
Offshore centres	6.8	2.6	4.1	1.8	1.5	0.4	0.4	
Developing countries	9.6	13.1	10.1	11.7	2.5	5.5	1.1	
Asia and Pacific	6.1	8.1	2.5	10.9	2.0	2.6	0.5	
Europe	0.5	1.1	1.7	–	0.3	–	–	
Latin America and Caribbean	1.3	2.3	3.3	–	–	0.6	0.6	

Source: Bank for International Settlements.

launched numerous retail products to satisfy the huge demand. Another factor during this period was the consolidation of the major banks, brokers and even fund management companies into the so-called 'bulge bracket banks' where being big was essential because the investment business just grew and grew, becoming totally global in its extent. While the volumes of business, the fees and the profits were there it was not a problem. As the markets slowed and then went into retreat the bulge bracket banks were left with a massive cost base and not enough business to pay for it. More consolidation followed but now it was more to remove an organization and reduce the number competing for dwindling business rather than to grow by expansion of the business.

The terrible events of 11 September 2001 would also have a profound effect not only on the already weak equity markets but also on everybody associated with the industry and beyond it as well. The sickening events, which evolved before the eyes of the world, were compounded by the possibility that the perpetrators had also profited by utilizing an aspect of equity markets, which means they will react to good and bad news, and today do so with great speed. Immediately the news broke the markets fell significantly as traders tried to work out the implications of what was happening in terms of world security and economies. Had the terrorists profited by selling shares in, for instance, airlines prior to committing the atrocity? Was this the most horrendous example of 'insider dealing' imaginable? Thankfully it seems that this did not happen and equally events such as 11 September are not common.

For operations teams the volatility and diverse nature of the equity markets presents a challenge different from that experienced by bond and money-market settlement teams. Most equities settle on a T + 3 or longer convention and the securities are very often registered rather than in bearer form. Delays in settlement of transactions cause problems and these are overcome by the application of various courses of action such as stock borrowing. A strategy may take several transactions to complete over several days and at different prices.

Transactions may be cumulative ('cum') or excluding ('ex') a benefit, action or distribution and while this is also the case with bonds, there are potentially more types of events with less predictability in equities.

The trading process in equities may be via an order book, face to face on a market floor, by telephone with a counterparty, etc. but it is important to remember that there are still events that can occur post a transaction, which require a decision from the front office or the client or operations and often all these parties. We have mentioned corporate actions or events and this is where there is still considerable work to be done in respect of, for instance, a rights issue.

A rights issue is where the company is seeking to raise additional capital by offering to sell more shares in the company. Under the pre-emptive right of shareholders in the UK these additional shares must be offered first to the existing shareholders. They have the right to take up those shares by paying the call or value to the company. Alternatively they can sell the rights to the new shares to someone else who will then pay the call or they can let the rights offer lapse and opt not to take up or sell the rights. They could also sell enough of the rights to the new shares, to take up some of the new shares at no cost.

Rights issue timetable

Distribution of nil-paid rights to shareholders on the register on record date
Decision to take up, sell or let rights lapse
Instructions to custodians/agents
Acceptance deadline
Call payment of the fully paid rights and payment of the lapsed rights
Pari passu from fully paid rights to ordinary shares

Rights are usually priced at a discount to the current market price, have a set period when the rights issue will close and a date on which the call becomes payable. Each stage is important and will require close liaison between the dealer or client and the operations team and in turn between operations and any custodians.

Other types of corporate action associated with equities include:

- a bonus issue of shares whereby the company issues new shares to existing shareholders for free in order to reduce the share price and make it more attractive to new investors (see example below)
- A merger or de-merger where new shares and/or cash is offered and replaces the existing shares
- A take-over where again shares and/or cash is offered and will replace existing shares if the takeover bid is successful or
- A capital restructure where the company might, for instance, offer to buy back some of its shares or to alter the nominal value of existing shares to perhaps return cash to shareholders.

Each action or event has deadlines, decisions, instructions and processing that require careful management. If an event occurs when

Example

ABC plc 2 for 3 bonus issue

ABC has a share price of £15 and decides to make a 2 for 3 scrip or bonus issue. A shareholder has 3000 shares so their position will be:

Before scrip issue	3000 shares @ £15	£45 000
Scrip	2000 shares -	-
After scrip issue	5000 shares	£45 000

Effective share price is now £9 (called the *ex-scrip* price)

the ownership of the shares has yet to be registered by the buyer, the existing holder named on the company register will receive the results of the event, likewise if the security has been lent to someone who has registered the security in their name or passed it onto another party. In these cases the benefit due on the action or event must be claimed by the beneficial owner, i.e. the rightful owner of the shares from the party that currently has legal ownership but not beneficial ownership.

Equity markets are very different from debt markets in the way in which they operate, the characteristics of the products, the strategies and, of course, the dealing and settlement conventions. We look again at some of these aspects of equity markets in later chapters. Operations teams need to understand how equities behave to be able to develop the systems, the procedures and the controls for such business. If they can do this they will reduce the scope for errors that inevitably cost money and reduce the profitability of the trades. Those errors also create another risk problem – reputation. Firms operating in equities are usually well aware of the counterparties that are good at the trading and settlement of transactions and those that are not!

In this chapter we have again only scratched the surface of the markets and in particular the intricacies of trading and investing in equities. What we have seen, however, is that there are many aspects of equities which require operations teams to understand the influence of market and economic trends on the levels of trading volume and additional activity like corporate actions. It is also important to understand the way in which equity products and derivative products are linked, so let us now consider the derivatives markets.

Chapter 4

Derivatives and commodities markets

If equity markets are diverse, derivatives markets are even more so. Innovative risk management tools, a speculator's dream, is one of many expressions used to describe derivatives and for a long time in the late twentieth century many were not particularly complimentary! Strange that this should be the case given that the purpose of a derivative product is to transfer risk from a party wishing to remove a risk to a party willing to take on the risk with a view to making a profit. Derivatives bring stability to all types of markets, reducing the need to sell assets and commodities in falling markets by preventing losses when such a fall occurs. As long ago as the Middle Ages derivative-type transactions took place so the product is not new. In 1848 the derivative markets we see today really began when the Chicago Board of Trade was established and standardized contracts, called futures, for commodities were created.

The standardization of the terms of a transaction into a contract enabled that contract to be freely traded. If a farmer purchased a grain contract he could subsequently sell this to someone else and remove the obligation created by the trades by having an offsetting long and short position, which could be closed out. As contracts were for the delivery of grain and were a legally binding obligation to do so on both the buyer and the seller this was an important feature. So too was the guarantee offered by the clearing house of the exchange which ensured that delivery would be honoured and that the grade of commodity delivered would meet the required specification. Coupled with the ability to discover the true price of the commodity as buyers and sellers gathered to trade on the market floor generating liquidity, it was of little surprise that success came quickly and within years other similar markets trading a range of commodities opened in the USA.

The scene remained much the same until the mid-1970s when financial futures contracts were introduced. From then on volumes of contracts traded on exchanges, which now numbered hundreds and were worldwide, grew at a fantastic rate. By the end of 2001 volumes were over 3 billion and rising. It is important to recognize that derivatives are not just traded on exchanges. In fact prior to 1848 'derivatives' were traded in the form of forward contracts and options. They were deals made between two parties and were transacted off-exchange, in other words there were no rules or regulations governing the deal and the terms were simply negotiated to suit both parties. While this type of trade was common there were large, and growing problems, with one or other party defaulting on their obligations and also with establishing the 'true' price for the deal. The Chicago Board of Trade was established to remove these problems and did so with the introduction of the standardized futures contract, which we recognize today.

The problem, if that is the right word, with derivatives is that when use of them is made without understanding what they are designed to do, or when their use is unauthorized or uncontrolled, then losses can and do occur. However, we should focus on the positive side of derivatives while respecting the need to understand the characteristics and potential risk associated with the product.

Derivatives transfer risk from those who wish to avoid or disperse the risk to those who wish to assume the risk with a view to profiting from the characteristics. With that basic concept we need to understand why the product is attractive to both hedgers (those who wish to get rid of risk) and speculators who wish to profit from their use.

A derivative is a generic term covering many different types of products. Derivatives also fall into those traded on exchanges and those traded off exchange or over-the-counter. OTC products, as the off-exchange version are called, are generally a more technical product used mainly by institutions and banks. Typically they will be designed for the specific strategy that the bank or institution requires and are therefore bespoke products. As such, a key element of the trading and settlement of this type of product is the detail of the transaction itself and the confirmation of the details with the counterparty to the trade, whereas those derivatives traded on an exchange assume the details of the contract specification of the product. In other words the exchange product is standardized and this allows the contracts to be bought and sold in the secondary market whereas this is very difficult and in many cases impossible with a bespoke OTC product that will have little general appeal. Table 4.1 and Figure 4.1 illustrate the details of an OTC interest rate swap transaction and an on-exchange equity stock option traded on LIFFE, the London International Financial Futures and Options Exchange.

Table 4.1 IRS confirmation for a transaction

Confirmation from Mega Bank	**To: Interbank Inc**
Interest Rate swaps	
Transaction Date	19/06/2001
Effective Date	21/06/2001
Maturity Date	21/12/2001
Terms	ISDA
Currency/Amount	UDS 5,000,000
We pay	5.76%
Frequency	Annual
Calculation Basis	Actual/365
We receive	6-Month LIBOR
Frequency	Semi-annual
Calculation Basis	Actual/360

Source: DMS Ltd.

Unit of trading:	One option normally equals rights over 100 or 1000 shares*, depending on the underlying share
Expiry months:	January Cycle (J): means the 3 nearest expiry months from Jan, Apr, Jul, Oct cycle February Cycle (F): means the 3 nearest expiry months from Feb, May, Aug, Nov cycle March Cycle (M): means the 3 nearest expiry months from Mar, Jun, Sep, Dec cycle
Exercise:	Exercise by 17:20 on any business day, extended to 18:00 for all series on a Last Trading Day
Last trading day:	16:30 (London time) – Third Wednesday in expiry month
Settlement day:	Settlement Day is four business days following the day of exercise/Last Trading Day
Quotation:	pence/share
Minimum price movement:	0.5 pence/share
Tick size & value:	Normally £0.50 or £5.00 depending on the underlying share
LIFFE CONNECT™ Trading hours:	08:00 – 16:30 (London time)
Contract standard:	Delivery will be 100 or 1000 shares (depending on the underlying share). This number may be amended by the Exchange following a corporate action.
Option premium:	Is payable in full by the buyer on the business day following a transaction.
Exercise price and exercise price intervals:	The interval between the exercise prices is set according to a fixed scale determined by the Exchange.
Introduction of new exercise prices:	Additional exercise prices will be introduced after the underlying share price has exceeded the second highest, or fallen below the second lowest, available exercise price.

* Due to corporate action contract adjustments some equity options series may have a non-standard contract size. Click here for details of unusual contract sizes.

Figure 4.1 A LIFFE website for individual equity option products

An IRS confirmation for a fixed/floating transaction would contain information as shown in Table 4.1. There are other items of information that can or will be added to this such as frequency being modified following convention.

Derivatives do something in the future, which is why some of the products like forwards and futures are given their names. The future may be a day, a week, a month, a year or many years.

The swap illustrated here is for five years and involves the swapping of fixed- and floating-rate interest flows. The option contract when it is first listed is for 9 months and is for the buyer a right to either take delivery of the shares (a *call* option) or to make delivery of the shares (a *put* option).

In the case of the swap the payer of the floating and receiver of the fixed flows is expecting interest rates to rise. While protecting the cost of the borrowing they have from an increase in interest rates they are also exposing themselves to a higher borrowing cost if in fact interest rates fall. They are taking a view of interest rates and are not really hedging a position as they could end up with much higher costs. The buyer of a *put* option, on the other hand, may be doing so either to hedge or to speculate. If they have a holding of the shares and purchase a *put* option they are doing the trade to create a hedge because the *put* option will increase in value if the share price falls, therefore offsetting the loss on the shares. If the share price should rise the cost of buying the *put* can be likened to an insurance premium and will be deducted from the profit the price increase generates on the stock.

If the buyer of the *put* has no holding of stock then they are speculating on a fall in the share price. If this happens then the price of the *put* will increase and the option can be sold at a profit. If it doesn't then the speculator will most likely lose their money. However, they will not have lost more than the cost of buying the right to sell, which is a fraction of the full value of the shares. Figure 4.2 illustrates the profit/loss profiles for the option trade described above and also for the purchase of a *call* option.

It is important to understand the basic characteristic of derivatives which, by definition, is 'an instrument that derives its value from or has its value linked to some other asset'.

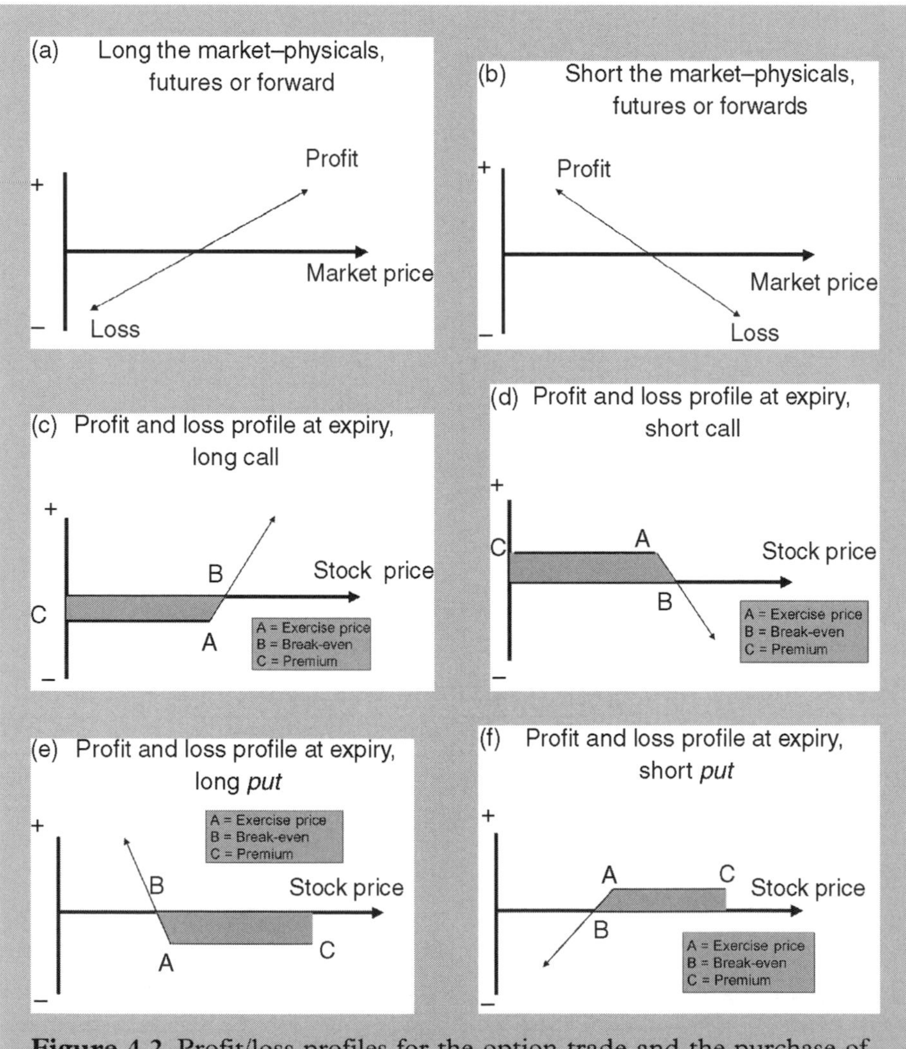

Figure 4.2 Profit/loss profiles for the option trade and the purchase of a call option. (Source: DMS Ltd)

Derivatives are quite separate instruments from those underlying assets as they are called but obviously they are closely linked to those assets and their price or value will change according to change in the price of the underlying asset. Crucially a derivative has a defined life and will mature at some stage and its value reflects the amount of time to maturity. This concept is readily understood in, say, bond markets but may be less of an obvious issue to those operating in the equity markets where shares usually have no set lifespan.

Above we also noted that the buyer of an option did not pay the full value that the option contract represented and this is another crucially important characteristic of most derivatives, and must be fully understood. Later in the chapter we look at this issue and see how it provides cost-effective hedging and at the same time is very attractive to the speculator by enabling leverage or gearing, simply the ability to gain a greater exposure to an asset through derivatives for a given capital outlay.

The seller, referred to as a writer or granter of the option, is in the position of receiving the amount paid for the right by the buyer, called the option premium, but that is the maximum profit they can make. Therefore it follows that the maximum loss the buyer can make is the amount of option premium paid.

A futures contract is a legally binding obligation to deliver an underlying commodity or asset. It is different from an option contract in that its profit/loss profile moves in a straight line similar to that of the underlying asset itself (see below). It is therefore a synthetic form of the underlying asset and can be used in many different strategies. The advantage of the future contract is that, like options, the full value of the contract is not paid unless delivery takes place. Thus the buyer of a FTSE 100 index futures contract is buying an exposure to the FTSE 100 index and will participate in any rise or fall in the index. However, they have not incurred the financial outlay that buying the equivalent value of the index in shares would have generated.

A speculator can gain a far greater exposure to the FTSE 100 index buying futures contracts with the available funds. The size or value and FTSE Index future represented is calculated, like all index futures, by multiplying the index level by the multiplier amount as per the contract specification published by the exchange. In this case the multiplier is £10 × the index so that at a level of 5250 each futures contract would represent £52 500 of exposure to the index.

If we apply this concept to options, the speculator that has, say, £10 000 to invest and believes the shares of BP Amoco are set to rise can either buy the shares or alternatively buy the right to take delivery of the shares through the purchase of *call* options. Look at the possible outcome in the following example.

Example

BP share price 364p and the 3-month 360 *call* options (1000 shares per contract) are priced at 85p so speculator can

1 Buy 2700 shares for £9828 plus commission
2 Buy 11 (£10 000/85p × 1000) of the 360 *call* options for £9350 plus commission (11 × 85p × 1000)

Assume in 3 months' time BP Amoco shares are trading at £5. What is the profit for each deal?

1 2700 shares purchased at £3.64 now worth £5 profit = 2700 × 136p = £3672
2 Eleven contracts purchased at 85p now priced at 140p (500 – 360) = 11 × 1000 × 55p = £6050

For an outlay of around £10 000 the speculator using options had bought an exposure to 11 000 BP Amoco shares and consequently made more money than had the £10 000 been used to purchase the shares outright. The speculator geared his position to get the greater exposure. However, there was a very great risk.

Suppose the share price of BP Amoco in 3 months' time is £3.00. The 360 *call* options will be worthless and the speculator has lost the £10 000, however the speculator that purchased the shares has lost 64p but still has the stock and the price could, of course, rise in the future and the shareholder gets any dividend paid, which, as they own options not shares, the option holder does not.

Gearing works both ways!

It is important to realize that gearing is only one attraction of using derivatives and many strategies used are in fact quite conservative and have a known loss, or are hedging which of course, is reducing risk not increasing it.

Table 4.2 gives the risk/reward profiles of the basic futures and options positions.

The use of derivatives is therefore widespread with private investors typically buying call options or writing (selling) call options against shares they hold while institutions will use a variety of products and strategies to hedge portfolios, gain exposures and manage asset allocations within portfolios.

Table 4.2 Summary of risk

Position	Risk	Reward
Long call	Limited to premium	Unlimited
Long put	Limited to premium	Almost unlimited
Short call	Unlimited (unless covered)	Limited to premium
Short put	Almost unlimited	Limited to premium
Long future	Almost unlimited	Unlimited
Short future	Unlimited	Almost unlimited

Source: DMS Ltd.

The market structure for exchange traded and OTC products is shown in Figure 4.3. For clients dealing in exchange traded derivatives, the trading and the settlement are divorced so that a variety of executing brokers can be used but all the business is settled through one counterparty. Costs and some elements of risk are better managed this way, as the essential element with derivatives trading is that the transactions and positions need to be confirmed and reconciled immediately. If they are not then the possibility of incorrect trades and unidentified positions (exposures) existing is very real. Many of the well-documented losses in derivatives resulted from 'hidden' positions by rogue traders, in other words it was the internal controls and procedures, and not the derivative products, which were to blame.

Derivatives markets exist in all the major financial centres and are diverse in nature with some specializing in particular products and others being multi-product based. Some exchanges focus on domestic products and users while others are international in their product line and membership.

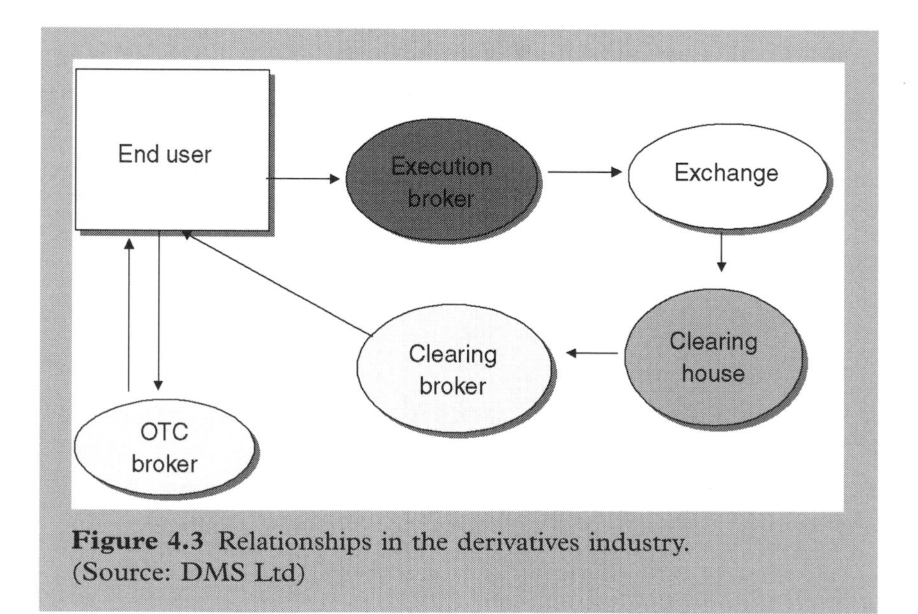

Figure 4.3 Relationships in the derivatives industry. (Source: DMS Ltd)

The evolution of the derivatives industry has seen old exchanges diversify and change in response to the introduction of new exchanges and, of course, to the changing requirements of the users of derivatives. For instance, the Chicago Board of Trade (CBOT), the oldest derivative exchange, has its origins heavily in commodities like grain but today trades a diverse mix of commodities and financial instruments. The CBOT is still an open-outcry market but has also introduced technology so that electronic and face-to-face trading takes place.

The CBOT has seen other exchanges such as LIFFE make the move to electronic trading after years of successfully operating in the open-outcry format. LIFFE was set up as a financial derivatives exchange trading futures and options on futures. It responded to the development, and the threat, of EUREX, the combined German/Swiss derivatives exchanges by abandoning open-outcry and developing its highly regarded LIFFE CONNECT trading system. But LIFFE also underwent other changes, absorbing the London Traded Option Market from the Stock Exchange and also the London Commodities Exchange to diversify into other products. More recently in October 2001 LIFFE announced its intention to join EURONEXT, itself a combination of the French, Belgian and Dutch bourses, in preference to accepting a bid from the London Stock Exchange.

London is in fact the home to several derivative exchanges including the London Metal Exchange and the International Petroleum Exchange; both are leading commodity markets with a very heavy international source of business and also the London Securities and Derivatives Exchange (OMLX). Returning to the CBOT, it has seen its long-held 'largest derivatives exchange in the world' tag move to EUREX and now it has for the first time been surpassed in the USA by its old rival the Chicago Mercantile Exchange (CME). Meanwhile also in Chicago the options exchange, set up by the CBOT in 1973, has seen record volumes in equity and index options. The Chicago Board Options Exchange (CBOE) has grown steadily through the last decade of buoyant equity markets and traded some 254 323 905 contracts[1] in 2001.

In the Asia–Pacific region growth and change have been the order of the day as mature derivatives markets in Singapore and Hong Kong merged with their relevant stock exchanges and 'new' markets like the options traded on the Korea Stock Exchange quickly established high volumes. Japan also has mature derivatives markets at the Tokyo Stock Exchange, OSAKA and the Tokyo International Financial Futures Exchange (TIFFE) as well as specialist and successful commodity markets like the Tokyo Commodity Market (TOCOM). A list of major derivatives markets is provided in Appendix 3 but beware, so much change and in particular mergers are happening all the time that an exchange can be here today and somewhere else tomorrow!

For some time now it has been possible to simultaneously trade in a security and a relevant derivative even though the two products trade on different exchanges. This type of arrangement can be illustrated by looking at the facilities currently offered by LIFFE to its members in the following example.

Example

LIFFE's Basis Trading Facility (BTF) introduced in 1995 was the first of its kind in Europe. It permits market users to enter into a conditional transaction involving both a LIFFE futures contract and a corresponding cash instrument.

To offer greater flexibility to the wholesale market, and in response to continued market demand, this facility has been extended over time to LIFFE's bond and swap futures, equity index futures and short-term interest rate (STIR) futures

[1] FOW Tradedata

contracts. A wide range of cash and OTC instruments are now eligible to form the cash leg of a Basis Trade involving LIFFE's futures contracts.

Source: LIFFE.

The merger of exchanges can, of course, pose problems initially for the teams dealing with clearing and settlement, although in the longer term it actually reduces the number of counterparties as the clearing and settlement processes are consolidated in the merged exchange's clearing house. There are even more benefits to be had if the clearing and settlement of securities and derivatives transactions becomes merged into a single entity. This is certainly beginning to happen with some markets and even where there is not a formal merger of the clearing houses, facilities are being provided that benefit the trading on an exchange. London has a prime example of that with the London Clearing House providing a central clearing counterparty function to CREST, which is the clearing house for the London Stock Exchange. As a result some trades can be executed with complete anonymity for both parties to the trade and eventually the settlement of trades will be netted bringing further benefits.

Commodity derivatives are traded on a wide range of underlying products. These are often put into categories such as 'softs', 'precious metals', 'energy' etc. There are so many different types of commodities on which there are derivatives that it is impossible to list them all here. However, some of the leading products are as follows:

Listed energy contracts

Exchange	**Contract**
Nymex	Light sweet crude oil 1000 bbl
IPE	Brent crude 1000 bbl
Tocom	Gasolene 100 kl

Listed softs/other contracts

Exchange	Contract
CboT	Corn 5000 bu
CboT	Soybean 5000 bu
TGE	Corn 100 000 kg

Listed metal contracts

Exchange	Contract
LME	Aluminium 25 tonnes
LME	Copper 25 tonnes
Tocom	Platinum 500 g
Tocom	Gold 1 kg

(*Source:* FOW TradeData)

Pricing derivatives is complex, and the more complex the derivative, the more intricate the pricing becomes. The price of a futures contract revolves around the fair value today for something that will be delivered in the future and the difference in the cost of purchase and therefore use of funding compared to buying the underlying (often referred to as the cost of carry). For commodities there are also issues like transportation, storage and warehousing costs. The price of an option takes into account that something will be delivered in the future but as there are different prices (strike or exercise prices) for that potential delivery each option has a different value and the price of the option moves by different amounts in response to a movement in price of the underlying asset. In both cases time has a value, but, of course, a diminishing value as the derivative moves closer to its maturity date. The longer to maturity, the more time value there is and so the price of an option with a strike price of 500 with 3 months to maturity will be less expensive than an option with the same strike price but 6 months to maturity.

Volatility and supply and demand also impact on prices and today dealers use pricing models to establish their estimate of the price a derivative should be that takes into account the cost of carry, implied volatility, theoretical prices, projected interest rates, etc. Incorporated into option pricing is what is referred to as the 'Greeks'. This is the measurement of the way in which an option price should change given a movement in the underlying, another measurement or time. Simply put, we have 'delta' the amount an option price should change given a one-point change in the underlying which can be between 0 and 1. A delta of 0.5 would mean that if the underlying moved by 10p the option price would change by 5p, a delta of 1 and the option would change by 10p. We also have 'gamma' which is the rate at which the delta changes and 'theta' the amount by which the option price changes because of the erosion of time value.

Delta is also used to work out the amount of hedge required. Market-makers make two-way (bid and offer) prices and are committed to buy and sell on those prices. Therefore they sometimes go short or sell option contracts they do not own. If the options are *calls* and are due to expire in, say, 6 months the market-maker is unlikely to need to deliver the shares (if it were an equity option) until near expiry day. Of course, the market-maker will only have to deliver the shares if the option has value on expiry by being in-the-money. Therefore today the market-maker does not need to fully hedge against that possibility and in fact will only start to buy the shares needed to meet the obligation if the share price rises above the strike price of the option and will do so as the delta tells him that delivery is becoming more likely. On expiry an in-the-money option will have a delta of 1 because the option will be exercised and delivery will take place. Conversely, an out-the-money option will have a delta of 0 as the option will not be exercised.

OTC derivatives are often priced using models for the simple reason that they will have tailored terms. The price of a standardized 1000 shares per contract 6-month BP Amoco *call* option with a strike price of 360 traded on LIFFE will be determined by the bids and offers input by the market participants. However, the price for a BP Amoco *call* option on 1 350 000 shares with a maturity two years away at a strike price of 354p and cash settled rather than the shares being delivered is negotiated between the buyer and seller.

We need to remember that OTC derivatives typically include swaps, forward rate agreements (FRAs), options (often referred to as exotic options because they have special conditions attached to them so we have, for instance, *barrier options* which are activated or cease to exist when a certain price is reached), credit derivatives etc. and in each case there is no exchange-generated contract specification to determine the terms of the derivative and the settlement. Understanding the contract specifications and settlement convention for exchange traded derivatives is vital and so it is for OTC trades as well except here the only means of getting that detail is via a confirmation from the counterparty that can be compared to the terms received from the dealer.

The growth in the use of OTC derivatives in the late 1900s was certainly helped by the introduction of standardized documentation to cover transactions. Today many OTC derivatives are entered into under the standard terms and conditions set out in the International Swaps and Derivatives Association (ISDA) Master Agreements. Until the Master Agreement was introduced, each OTC transaction needed to have an agreement drawn up and agreed by the legal departments in each of the counterparties to the trade. Naturally enough, this was time consuming and expensive and restricted the amount of business being transacted in this way. The agreements, of course, were crucial as an OTC transaction is essentially a credit risk on each of the parties to the trade and there are no exchange rules or regulations that determine the terms of the trade and, more importantly, unlike exchange-traded derivatives, no clearing house guaranteeing the trade. Today this risk is reduced in some cases by the provision of a central clearing counterparty that becomes the guarantor to each side of the trade in a similar way to the exchange traded deal. The London Clearing House provides just such a facility to its members through its SwapClear and RepoClear products.

The confirm to an OTC trade becomes an important document enabling verification of the trade details. Any discrepancy needs to be advised to the front office and resolved quickly with an amended confirm sent to the counterparty. The operations function provides an important control feature to OTC trading which would otherwise present a significant risk to a firm.

Derivatives markets are often fast-moving as volatility in the derivative can be greater than that of the underlying. OTC transactions can be very complex but equally can be simple in design and are often for very large values. Many of the main exchange products are popular with good liquidity, depending on the type of OTC. Derivative liquidity can be less good, and offer a relatively cheap way into the market or a simple hedging mechanism.

Trading derivatives is, like debt, money market and equity products, a core activity in the financial markets. We have looked at some strategies for using more than one type of product and although many outside the industry might not recognize it, derivatives are often being utilized in their savings, mortgage or investment products. Retail markets are where many products that use bonds, equities and derivatives exists so let us now look into the world of investment and retail products more closely.

Chapter 5

Trading, dealing and investment

The 'dealing room' is to many people what the financial markets are all about. A noisy, pressure-filled place where only a 'certain' type of person can survive and, until comparatively recently, that meant mean, confident, strong-willed, young, men mis-behaving!

This kind of image and generalization is, not surprisingly, far off the mark. Yes, there are many young, arrogant and noisy dealers, but that is hardly unique to financial markets, and the antics of certain professional footballers and offspring of the famous spring to mind. Certainly, some dealers are known to 'relax' by playing hard in the clubs and bars but then the demands of their particular job requires a release of the pressure to perform aggressively and successfully for many hours. Equally, in the heat of the moment as the success of the deal varies, an outpouring of emotion is hardly surprising. OK so the language may be bad and the humour often tasteless to the 'average' person, but then if you cannot handle that you shouldn't be on the dealing floor or, for that matter in a job, which means you potentially come into contact with that kind of environment. In any case, not all dealers or dealing rooms possess these characteristics. Many are full of decent hard-working and pleasant men and women doing their job and having good and bad days at the office, exactly the same as the operations teams in the middle and back offices!

Of course, to those who have to liaise with the dealers in this supposedly raucous environment, it can be somewhat daunting, particularly for new or junior personnel. A problem can exist in terms of the relationship between the so-called front office and those supporting that function in the middle and/or back offices. If the relationship issue becomes too significant it impacts across the business. What causes the relationship between dealers and operations to be really good or bad or even in between?

There are many possibilities. Certainly a lack of understanding of the role of each area, the processes, critical times and failure to appreciate the importance of a request or piece of information will not make for much mutual respect. Operations teams need to understand the dealing environment, the important issues and the pressure. By doing so they can communicate better and from a position of confidence and that will be appreciated. The dealers are essentially a client and a very important one at that. Of course, that does not make them always right, nor does it require total subservience, in fact exactly the opposite is needed. However, there is no doubt that a firm with a front office and operations team that have mutual respect for each other, has understood the working environment and the requirements that each area has and can genuinely work together, will be highly successful.

It is therefore important for an operations team to understand the basics: for instance, in the dealing area there are differing roles and ways of actually trading. There are principal traders dealing with the firms' own money, arbitrageurs trying to profit from price anomalies, market-makers quoting bid and offer prices in amounts which they are committed to trade and sales teams executing orders on behalf of clients. The dealers in a fund management organization will be operating very differently from a principal trader at a major international bank, the latter being often referred to as traders. Dealers or traders in different types of products have markets, which can be more or less volatile than others and consequently are more or less difficult to trade in. Dealers on the sales desk are operating for clients trying to achieve the best price and get paid a commission while traders have profit targets to hit if their bonus is to top up their basic pay. There is pressure on both, but it is a different pressure. Likewise, the skill sets are different and so, often, is the character of the person.

It is essential for operations personnel and particularly managers and supervisors to understand the trading and dealing they support. By recognizing what is going on in the pre-trade and trading environments they will be better able to provide the services that are needed and also to cope with the occasional outbursts and stress on the relationship between what is, after all, two integrally linked business units which need each other. The front–back office relationship is vital to the overall success of the company. Without a good understanding of each other's roles there is potential for significant risk situations to develop and the likelihood of financial loss through unnecessary errors and inefficiencies. Just as importantly, there is the risk of breaching regulations, hidden dealing, incorrect positions and compliance failures, all of which will have very significant consequences for the firm should they occur. If we look at the issues that arise in trading and dealing we can see where the potential for problems lies.

Whatever is transacted in the marketplace has to be settled. This fundamental premise illustrates that the operations function is important to the front office otherwise any profit the dealer makes will not be realized. The efficient recording of the transactions and their reconciliation to the market are vital. The information on open positions, status of trades and whether a purchased security has been received and is therefore available to be sold and delivered on, will enable the front office to avoid transactions that may incur costs as well as to take advantage of opportunities safe in the knowledge that their dealing position is confirmed and correct. Suffice to say that if the information is late and/or error-strewn the dealer can lose confidence and be reluctant to take new positions until the true position is confirmed. Losses can occur on existing transactions because of late settlement, incorrect instructions and sundry other errors. Additional costs and expenses including possible fines levied by the exchange and or regulators are a real possibility. These costs reduce the profit or increase the loss on the trades, making the dealers' job harder and will not endear the operations team to them.

The traders therefore rely on operations teams to check, verify and record the trade details and to reconcile the positions held on the book. Traders and dealers assume that the transactions they enter into are OK, but only the matching process confirms this is the case. Matching processes differ depending on the type of market. Open-outcry markets generate potential unmatched or 'out-trades' because of the face-to-face dealing process where there is scope for misunderstanding and error. Electronic markets, on the other hand have no mismatches as the system can only carry out trades where the details match. There is a point here to remember, of course, and that is that a trader or dealer can still carry out an incorrect transaction, i.e. buying instead of selling in an electronic market and so from an operations point of view the traders and dealers records need verifying to the trades actually carried out. To illustrate the two types of market, open-outcry and electronic, Figure 5.1 shows a transaction in a futures contract on the exchange floor of the Chicago Board of Trade and Figure 5.2 an equity trade on the London Stock Exchange.

In Figure 5.1 the flow for transaction is relatively straightforward. Key points in the process are the order placing to the booth on the trading floor and the transmitting of the order to the trader in the pit or area designated for trading by the exchange. Once the trade is completed, which can be a matter of a few seconds, the order is confirmed as filled by the booth clerk. However, at this stage the trade is not matched. That will be the case after the details of the trade are compared to the details submitted by the counterpart to the trade. If everything agrees then matching is complete and the transaction passes to the clearing process for settlement. If it does not agree then the two parties to the trade must resolve the disputed details. On most markets there will be a strict deadline by which the unmatched trades must be resolved.

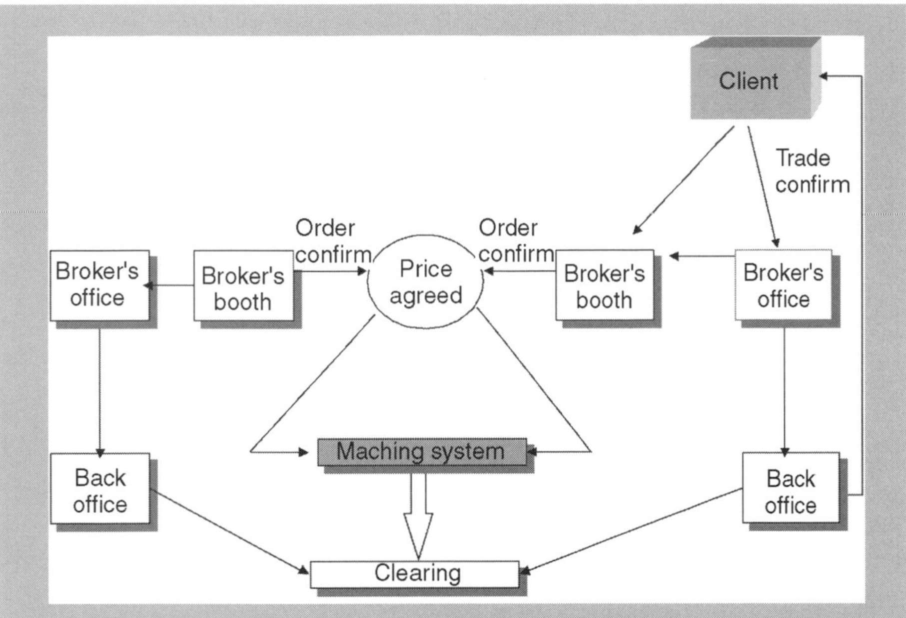

Figure 5.1 An open-outcry transaction at the Chicago Board of Trade (Source: DMS Ltd)

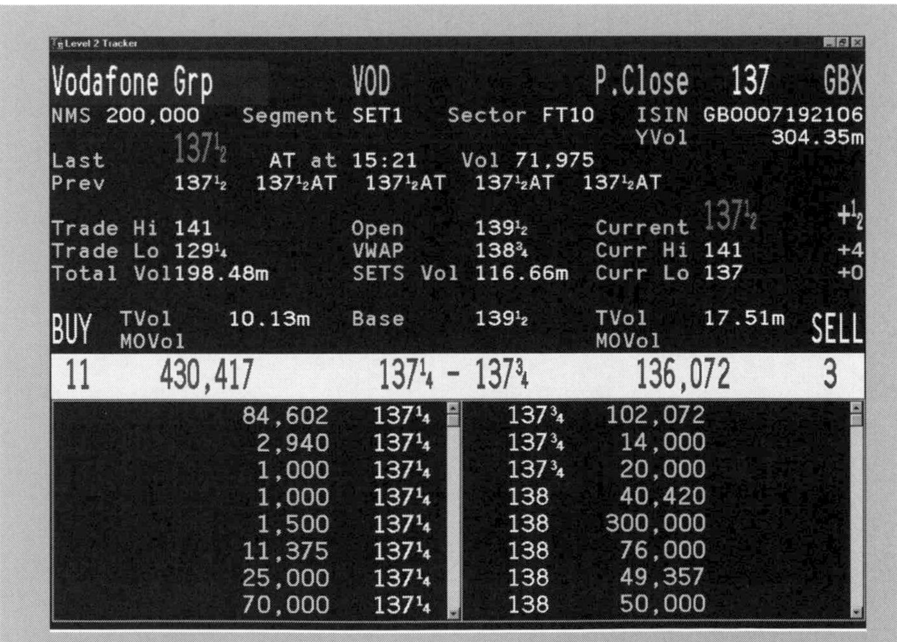

Figure 5.2 The electronic market process. (Source: The London Stock Exchange)

The electronic market process is somewhat different. The order is transacted on the system (as illustrated in Figure 5.2) and as the details of the order must agree for the trade to take place there is immediate matching.

Before a trade takes place, however, there are several key stages and issues to consider, one of them being the price. We have already touched on aspects of pricing in earlier chapters and know that in basic terms pricing is market-driven. Supply and demand dictate the price of goods and most financial instruments – a preponderance of sellers forces prices down and vice versa with buyers. But what makes people buy or sell?

Sometimes it is driven by need, for instance a grower of coffee beans will have the intention of selling these to a producer of coffee products. It can also be to realize a profit so that a buyer of shares at, say, 300p might sell them if the price reaches 500p. A fund manager receiving funds from investors will buy securities or other products for the portfolio. An example of this will be a unit trust manager. We cover retail products in some detail in Chapter 7 but it is worth considering here the general issues related to retail products and fund management dealing.

Unit trusts are collective investment schemes where the investment or subscriptions of many investors, who buy units in the fund, are pooled so that the maximum exposure to markets and securities for the invested amount can be achieved. If there are more buyers of units than sellers the fund manager has cash to invest. On the other hand, if there are more sellers of units then the manager must raise funds to settle the purchase of the units and does so by selling assets out of the portfolio.

The decision on which of the securities to buy or sell will rest on the performance of the investment. Thus a company that has cut its dividend due to poor results may find fund managers selling the stock and thus the price of the shares comes under pressure and may fall.

Historically fund managers have taken long-term views on investments, looking at the company's performance over several years rather than a few months or a year. However, growing competition in fund management and from other types of products has meant that managers will potentially be more active in adding and removing individual shares from their portfolios, trying to give the best return to investors and to attract more business. Some funds are called tracker funds and they, as the name implies, track something like an index, aiming to give the same or slightly better returns to the investor than they would have achieved had they bought the shares in the companies that make up, say, the FTSE 100 index. This buying and selling of securities by fund managers can be a substantial part of the activity in the individual securities and markets. For instance, an index tracker fund manager will buy the shares of companies about to be admitted to the index and sell the shares of those falling out of the index. Fund management dealing follows a process similar to that shown below:

1 Strategy policy meeting
2 Strategy decision
3 Authorization of strategy
4 Order construction and verification
5 Order placement to dealing desk
6 Order placed with broker
7 Transaction confirmed
8 Portfolio updated
9 Transaction and position reconciled by operations to broker statements

When we look at the volumes of business traded in markets liquidity is, as we have discovered, always important. The turnover in the trading of instruments also varies depending on the level of desire or need to trade so that some commodities trade heavily around planting and harvest times. Others like derivatives trade heavily when situations develop or look like developing and people want to either speculate or hedge the outcome. An example here would be the activity in short-term interest rate futures ahead of an expected or after an unexpected announcement by the central bank of a change in interest rates. Another example would be activity in oil derivatives or gold products at times of tension in say the Middle East, where any disruption of oil production and the possibility of conflict create enormous uncertainty for the world's commercial and financial markets.

Turnover or volume of activity therefore impacts on prices. It does so both because people are selling and buying and because the turnover itself generates what is known as liquidity. If liquidity, the amount of activity, is low then those wanting to buy will find that the price is at a premium. This can lead to problems, particularly if the purchase is needed to cover an obligation, for instance, to deliver the product as a result of a derivative position. Such situations have in the past caused serious problems for the authorities.

In the USA a situation developed in silver that led to legislation making 'cornering a market' an offence. What had happened to prompt such action? Two brothers purchased silver, so much in fact that there was little or none available in the market. At the same time they entered into derivative products that would require the sellers to deliver silver to them. As the maturity date approached and the sellers tried to buy silver they found none available except at hugely inflated prices. Likewise the derivatives were also at inflated prices making either the purchase of silver to deliver or the buying back of their obligations in the derivatives a transaction that would create a massive loss.

More recently the same happened in Germany, again involving an asset, in this case government bonds and the derivatives, bond futures. As maturity of the futures approached there were more bonds needed for delivery against the futures than bonds available in the market. A 'squeeze' occurred, creating artificially high prices in bonds that caused the German authorities to arrange for additional bonds to be available in the market and thus bring normality back to the prices.

Other factors affect pricing. We know some bonds and money-market instruments are issued at a discount so that the price on issue is well below the par value that will be paid on redemption. How is that discount arrived at? The investor and the issuer are concerned at the yield that the instrument will provide and how much it will cost the company to borrow the money. For the company they will receive, say, £75 and have to repay £100 in 5 years' time. It has cost them £5 per year to borrow £75 but they will only have to pay the total in 5 years' time. For the investor they are going to receive £25 profit in 5 years' time on an investment of £75. They will want to know what that is in terms of yield so that they can compare it to, say, putting £75 in a fixed-income bond with an interest rate of 5%.

The buyer of the fixed rate bond could, of course, invest the income each year and therefore the return on the investment would be higher.

So pricing is all about what something is worth today and what it will or may be worth in the future. It is a combination of cost of purchase against potential sale price or redemption value coupled with the possible income in terms of interest or dividend payment.

The value of a share as we saw in Chapter 3 is not easy to establish. The actual price may appear lower than another share but the potential for capital gain or maintained income from the dividend may not be so good as with a higher-priced share. Future earnings potential that is built into a price may not happen, as was graphically illustrated by many of the technology stocks of the late 1990s and early 2000s that soared in price on expectation rather than proven profitability and just as quickly collapsed when it became apparent that such earnings potential was not achievable. Why did the price soar so much then? The answer is simple: supply and demand. A momentum built up that became self-fuelling. As investors poured into technology stocks other investors became concerned that they would miss out on this sure-fire profit so they piled in, driving prices yet higher. This also happens with house prices. Of course, sooner or later the bubble usually bursts and many investors are left nursing large losses in their portfolios. It should also be remembered that it is not only the private investor who gets sucked into this crazy environment, many experienced bankers and fund managers were caught out by the dotcom craze and more recently by collapses like Enron.

Fund managers and principal dealers are judged on the profit or loss they make but their trading style is very different. For the principal trader the profit/loss judgement is based on targets set by the firm that they believe and expect to be achievable given certain conditions. The reason a loss may be acceptable is based on the assumption that certain markets are cyclical in the sense that they are more volatile at certain times, so they can therefore be difficult to operate in at times and yet the firm needs the capability to be able to trade in that market.

The term loss leader is used where losses in one market or product are accepted because a profit can be made elsewhere but it is dependent on the firm trading in the loss maker. Thus a dealer running a book in a difficult market or product will be judged to have performed excellently if they keep a loss on that book lower than expected. Their task may have been significantly more difficult than a dealer in a highly liquid stock where the opportunity to make profitable deals occurs all the time.

Fund managers seek to provide a return on the funds invested with them, which is competitive with other available investment opportunities and, of course, with similar funds. Independent Financial Advisers (IFAs) will analyse all the options available for their clients and recommend the most suitable and best-performing products. Underperforming funds will obviously suffer because investors will look to switch to better-performing alternatives. Equally, a pension fund manager must ensure that the fund not only meets the investment conditions and requirements but that it also meets its expected return against an agreed benchmark. Any failure to do this, particularly if it happens frequently, will result in the fund being moved to a new management company. Worse still, it could result in the pension fund going to court as happened when Unilever's Pension Fund sued its manager for alleged breaches of the management terms and failure to meet performance objectives.

Sales teams are assessed on the commission they generate from selling to their clients. Again the success or otherwise of the salesperson depends on the list of clients and the markets they trade. Some clients trade large orders in products where high levels of commission are charged, others trade many orders but in markets where commission rates are much lower. Dealers in a fund management company are neither principal traders nor salespersons. Their job is to carry out the trades for the strategies the fund managers wish to implement. Their skill is in placing the orders with the brokers and getting the best prices and commission rates as well as feeding back to the fund managers market information gleaned from the contacts at the brokers that is relevant to the strategies.

In order to service the fund management clients, the brokers' salesperson will sometimes deal with their principal dealers, particularly if there is some kind of complex deal to be done or the market is perhaps not liquid enough to enable them to complete the deal at the price the client wants. When a highly complex deal is sought by the client, specialist teams often work to provide the solution. Structured product teams will put together the deal often involving several separate transactions with different dealing books in the firm, for instance the bond desk, FX, swaps dealers and treasury. The resultant deal is often a unique product for that client, but equally the structured product teams also look to create a product that might appeal to fund managers and having developed such a product will then start to try to sell it to their clients. Other deals involve baskets of different securities, so rather than many individual transactions in shares a single basket of shares is traded as a single deal. However, for the operations teams at both the client and the broker there are still all the individual trades that make up the basket deal to be booked and settled through the accounts!

Whether they are principal traders, salespersons, structured product teams or dealers in fund management companies they are often under pressure. They also rely considerably on the efficiency of their colleagues in operations. How do operations teams support the dealers? Key support functions are:

- Trade capture and verification
- Position management
- Corporate action management
- Collateral management
- Stock lending and borrowing
- Accounting
- Record keeping
- Client services
- Reconciliation and controls
- Management information

Each of these processes is described in more detail in another title in this series and for operations teams these are core functions with which they will be familiar. The influences on these functions that come from the trading and dealing and from the markets themselves is the important issue. Trading, dealing and investment are very different disciplines that work in the same market environments. Likewise, the operational support for this activity is varied and yet closely linked in the post- and to some extent the pre-execution process. Today it is just as vital that operations understands the front-office process as it is to understand the clearing and settlement process.

Trading takes place on- and off-exchange so as part of the process of understanding trading and dealing it is important to recognize the role of the exchange. Therefore let us look at what exchanges do.

Chapter 6

The role of the exchange

The financial markets are divided into those where trading takes place under the rules and regulations of an organized market and those where the trading takes place over-the-counter. The role of the exchange is an important one as it provides not only facilities for trading but also end users with a degree of comfort that such trading is taking place in a regulated environment. From an operations point of view the structure of the exchange will provide the clearing organization and also the product specifications as well as essential data for the clearing and settlement processes.

An exchange first and foremost must gain regulatory approval. Part of that process will be to convince the authorities of the merits of the market and the strength of the rules governing participation in the market. The regulator grants approval in the UK by granting either designated or recognized status, so we have Recognized Investment Exchanges (RIEs). In the UK the following exchanges have attained the status. These are:

- The London Stock Exchange
- The London International Financial Futures and Options Exchange
- The London Metal Exchange
- International Petroleum Exchange
- OMLX – The London Securities and Derivatives Exchange

- virt-X
- COREDEAL
- Jiway

Overseas exchanges, which are not under the control of the FSA but where the FSA believes that their operation is such that it establishes fair prices, are given the status of Designated Investment Exchanges (DIEs). The status granted to an exchange has implications for investment by fund managers and investors, as, in many cases, the trustees for trading and investment would not approve an exchange without a status.

The role of the exchange is fundamentally different when it is a derivative rather than a securities exchange. The main difference is that a securities or stock exchange is where a company lists its shares or securities. This process of obtaining a listing is to raise finance by offering shares to the public, including institutions, in the primary market and then having those shares traded in the secondary market. Rules govern the listing of a company's shares. In the UK the listing authority used to be the London Stock Exchange but it is now the FSA.

Once a company's shares are listed, the exchange monitors the trading activity in the secondary market and ensures that the company is complying with the requirement to make available information of material interest to investors and shareholders. The information that a company must supply includes basic regulatory and legal requirements. This will include the date of the annual general meeting, production of the accounts, changes to board directors, buying or selling of shares by directors, major acquisitions or disposals that will impact on the company's performance and profit/loss account, etc. Any failure to comply with this will result in the exchange suspending the company's shares from trading. Equally, if the company is going to make an announcement related to the company's activities then it may seek a temporary suspension of its shares until the announcement is publicly made. Such instances would typically be a rights issue or recapitalization announcement, merger discussions, etc.

By way of illustration, an example of information of material interest would be when a listed football club makes a major signing or sells a leading player. The impact of the funding costs, cash receipts and impact on performance are all likely to affect the share price.

This suspension of a company's shares will also happen if, for instance, a company's share price moves significantly, indicating that rumours are circulating about an imminent announcement. It will also happen even if the company is unaware of any reason why there should be unusual activity in its shares or share price. The exchange or the company can suspend share trading and, from an operations point of view, it is essential to have data about suspended securities and also about any changes to the capital structure, dividends, etc.

A derivatives exchange, however, is very different. Here the products traded are not those listed by companies to raise finance but are products designed by the exchange. As we saw in Chapter 4, the standardized futures contract was established by the Chicago Board of Trade and standardized option contracts followed when the Chicago Board Options Exchange was established in 1973. Today these two exchanges are among the leading derivative exchanges in the world. The exchanges traded in excess of 3.5 billion contracts on a variety of products, each one designed by the exchange.

In general terms the role of the exchange is to:

- Gain regulatory approval
- Appoint a clearing organization
- Determine the rules and regulations of the exchange
- Establish the membership criteria
- Provide a trading mechanism(s)
- Supervise the trading activities
- Design products (derivatives exchanges)

- List products for trading (securities exchanges)
- Provide information
- Provide data on prices

Although individual exchanges are very different the above roles are standard around the world. We can see how an exchange is structured by taking as examples the London Stock Exchange and Euronext.

Brokers and jobbers formed the London Stock Exchange in around 1773. These jobbers (market-makers, as they would be termed today) met previously in coffee shops where business took place. The business transacted was in stocks and shares, much of which was in bearer form. The ownership of the stock or share was evidenced by the possession of a document, no central register of owners being maintained. Today, registered securities, mainly shares, will have a record of the owner of those shares maintained by a registrar appointed by the company.

The role of the stock exchanges in most of the countries has undergone significant change. A major alteration to the structure of many exchanges has been the replacement of face-to-face or open-outcry dealing with electronic and telephone dealing. The 'floor' of the exchange where brokers and jobbers/market-makers met to negotiate deals was limited by two key factors, capacity and international or global investment, both of which came about because of factors like the deregulation of financial markets. With major US and foreign banks joining to create global investment banks and technology providing information faster to participants, volumes of trades increased dramatically. The cost of maintaining teams of people proved a massive handicap to the large players and the inevitable switch to cheaper and faster electronic trading systems, as we have noted elsewhere, gathered pace.

However, it was not just a case of the method of dealing changing that has seen so much change to the structure of stock exchanges, particularly the London Stock Exchange. The competition from other types of market, particularly computerized trading systems and

Internet-based trading, together with the loss of the role of Listing Authority to the regulator, the Financial Services Authority and the settlement process to CREST Co. Ltd marked significant alterations to the role of the exchange. In addition, the London Traded Option Market moved to LIFFE although the LSE has introduced new markets like the Alternative Investment Market (AIM), TechMARK, etc. The loss of different roles has not, to date, altered the LSE's status as one of Europe's largest stock exchanges as we saw in Figure 1.3 (see Chapter 1).

Changes have also occurred to the way in which dealing is carried out on the LSE. Today trading in the leading shares takes place on the Stock Exchange Electronic Trading System (SETS), an order-driven market introduced in 1997. The computerized system matches buy and sell orders input by member firms. In another change to the way in which trades are dealt and processed today, the matched trade details are passed to the Central Counterparty Service (CCP) operated by the London Clearing House for CREST. The two parties to the trade settle with the CCP and so remain anonymous to each other. However, not all securities listed on the LSE trade via SETS.

SETS securities are FTSE 100 stocks, FTSE 100 reserve stocks, and any stocks which have been removed from the index and a number of other stocks with regular trading in reasonable size. Operationally this use of the CCP has removed the need to settle trades with the individual counterparties and this process is explained in greater detail in another book in this series.

The order book process is straightforward as the examples on pages 86 and 87 show.

How do trades in non-SETS securities take place? Non-SETS securities are traded using the Stock Exchange Automated Quotation System. Here market-makers' bids and offers are electronically displayed and to complete the deal the market-maker must be phoned to confirm the price and the trade is then completed.

Example

Limit order

Buy orders		Sell orders	
5 000	870	3 400	871
3 000	870	2 600	871
2 000	869	12 000	872
4 000	869	8 000	872

Limit Order is submitted to sell 14 000 shares at no less than 870.

- 8000 of the order is done automatically
- The single sell order is completed against two buy orders. This is known as a *multiple fill* and cannot be avoided
- The display now becomes:

Buy orders		Sell orders	
2 000	869	6 000	870
4 000	869	3 400	871
		2 600	871
		12 000	872
		8 000	872

Note: The 6 000 sell order displayed is the balance of the 14 000 limit order

Different markets have different trading processes. The New York Stock Exchange (NYSE) has a trading floor where all the transactions take place. There are twenty trading posts manned by a specialist and specialist clerks. Orders are given direct to the specialist (SuperDot system) or to brokers via telephone or the Broker Booth Support System (BBSS) and all trading takes place around these trading posts. The NYSE is a highly effective combination of face-to-face dealing and technology.

Example

At best order

Buy orders		Sell orders	
5 000	870	3 400	871
3 000	870	2 600	871
2 000	869	12 000	872
4 000	869	8 000	872

Order submitted to sell 6 000 at the best

- Order will be executed automatically
- The screen will now become:

Buy orders		Sell orders	
2 000	870	3 400	871
2 000	869	2 600	871
4 000	869	12 000	872
		8 000	872

Source: The Securities Institute

In Australia all trades in the ASX-listed equities take place on computers. Warrants, company options, interest rate securities and Exchange Traded Options are also traded on computers. Equities, warrants, company options and interest rate securities are traded on SEATS (Stock Exchange Automated Trading System), the Australian Stock Exchange's computerized trading system. Exchange Traded Options are traded on the Derivatives Trading Facility, which is a separate computer system.

Shares began to trade on SEATS in 1987 and by the end of 1990 all share trading on ASX was taking place on SEATS and the trading floors were closed. Members of the public do not have direct access to SEATS, but place orders on SEATS by telephoning their broker or by trading on-line. Brokers may use other systems for trading and orders from these systems are also passed through to SEATS.

SEATS matches buy and sell orders then trades them automatically. Best-priced orders have priority. If there is more than one order at the same price, the order which was placed first takes precedence. Large orders have no priority over small orders.

The exchanges described above are securities markets but what about other types of markets? Most significant of the non-securities are those which trade commodities and also the insurance market at Lloyd's of London. For good measure we can add in the Baltic Exchange as well. This book focuses on securities markets but it is good to reflect on these other important markets.

Lloyd's of London can be traced back to the days of Edward Lloyd's coffee house in the City of London, which was well known in business in 1688. The Society of Lloyd's was incorporated by the Lloyd's Act of 1871 and by 1900 Lloyd's was the international market for insurance risks of almost every type. People who underwrite insurance are called *names* and they join together to form *syndicates*. This has the effect of spreading risk as the underwriting is spread among many names. However, although there is the potential for a good return from the premiums paid to the syndicates there is still a risk of significant losses if a major insurance claim is made against a syndicate, which has a large exposure. Since 1994 companies have been able to become corporate names at Lloyd's.

There are many commodities markets around the world. Some we know are part of exchanges, which also trade other products like securities or financial derivatives. Some, though, are specialist markets like the New York Mercantile Exchange (NYMEX), the London Metal Exchange (LME), the Tokyo Commodity Exchange (TOCOM) and the International Petroleum Exchange (IPE).

Chapter 7

Fund management and retail markets

Fund management is obviously about managing funds and this can be, and often is, a combination of cash and vehicles for investment. Personal funds such as cash in hand and cash held in bank accounts can be committed, i.e. they are needed against known or expected expenditure and non-committed or excess cash that is not anticipated to be needed in the short to medium term to meet current or projected expenditure. The use which this excess cash can be put to is varied and could range from 'frivolous or fun spending' to investment designed to grow capital and possibly provide income. Almost certainly we would expect the investment to match or better the rate of inflation so that the value of the cash does not diminish.

How to manage that cash is the question, as most people are neither experienced in terms of markets and products nor, more importantly, do they have time to manage the investment. Equally important is the fact that most of us have relatively modest amounts to invest which makes an above-average return on the investment harder to achieve. As a result the fund management element of the financial services industry is growing rapidly as the growth in the economy and resulting wealth creation generates more funds that require management.

Funds allow the investments of individuals to be amalgamated or pooled so that the investment scope is greater. This is the aim of investment vehicles such as unit trusts and open-ended investment companies as well as investment trusts. Packaged products such as ISAs allow the investment in products such as unit trusts to be 'tax efficient'. To most people fund management is about the chosen organization managing the buying and selling of investments with our investment and making us a good return. In reality fund management is a complex function run as a business and comprising several different areas.

The role of the fund manager is indeed to manage the investment programme and we will see in some detail how that applies to unit trusts and other types of products such as ISAs. Packaged products is the term which is applied by regulators to a fund when it is a unit trust or life fund but the term also applies, along with 'wrapper', to the type of programme mentioned in the previous paragraph. Thus pension plans, mortgage repayment plans and ISAs are examples of packaged products.

The fund manager is an integral part of the money flow, taking cash from investors and placing that money into various products in the financial markets. Thus a venture capital fund is taking the investors' cash and providing capital to new companies through buying shares in the primary market. Where the type of fund is more conservative the fund manager is nevertheless providing support for businesses investing in the shares of companies and, when there is a rights issue for instance, supporting the company by taking up those rights and providing new capital.

Fund managers are not simply buyers of shares and while they are likely to take a medium- to long-term view on a company they may vary the holding of individual shares in order to retain balance in the portfolio or to ensure that investment objectives are met. This buying and selling of shares by fund managers provides vital liquidity in the secondary market. Most funds are themselves investments and therefore fund management is an investment business. In regulatory terms the Financial Services and Markets Act 2000 provides the instruments constituting 'investments' and the activities involving investments that constitutes investment business. The regulations also determine the legislation governing the establishment and operation of 'collective investment schemes', the term used to describe pooled funds organized as unit trusts or investment companies.

Investment business encompasses many types of products and providers. As we have mentioned elsewhere in this book, this includes:

- Banks
- Brokers
- Life insurers
- Pension scheme managers
- Investment houses
- Unit trust managers
- Trustees
- Custodians
- Nominee companies

Types of funds are usually easily identified from their title, which also invariably describes their purpose. For example, *Life Funds* are where the pool of money contributed to a life assurance company is invested for the purpose of providing benefits upon death or the expiration of the policy. The policies are, of course, denoting that the legal ownership of the investments acquired by the life fund vests with the life company and that the policies are the contracts with the ultimate beneficiaries. The payment of benefits is determined by the terms of each policy so that we have with-profits, fixed and guaranteed policies. The level of benefits for a with-profits policy is therefore very much dependent on the value and performance of the fund over the period or life of the contract. Many factors may also influence the value of benefits attributable to a particular policy.

Other common types of funds are:

- Pension funds
- Unit trusts
- Common investment funds
- Investment trusts
- Open-ended investment companies (OEICs)
- Offshore funds
- Venture capital trusts
- Private banking/portfolios

Some of these funds are referred to elsewhere in the book but it is worth revisiting the key points.

Pension funds denote that money contributed to a pension scheme has been invested to provide either an actual pension to participants on retirement or a sum of money that is used to buy an annuity. As the scheme may well be required to provide a payment for death in service benefit and widows' pensions it is often provided by a life company and linked to a life policy. There are, broadly speaking, two types of scheme: a defined benefits or final salary scheme or a money purchase scheme such as a personal pension. In the case of the defined benefits scheme the contributions can be made by the employee as well as the employer while in the money purchase scheme contributions are invested to grow into a sum of money which is realized at a future date and used to purchase an annuity (a stream of income). More recently stakeholder pension schemes have been introduced as a variant on personal pensions. Introduced in April 2001 they are viewed as important in the drive to ensure that an increasingly ageing population (it is estimated that in the UK there will be more pensioners than children for the first time ever by 2008) has adequate provision for their retirement. It is also becoming more common for companies to dispense with the costly final salary schemes, again causing concern that retirement provisions are not sufficient.

Unit trusts are the most common form of collective investment scheme, and are legally constituted as a trust with the purpose of providing income and/or capital growth. The portfolio of investments is acquired from the pool of invested funds contributed by the unit holders. The trustee is the legal owner of the investments and acts on instructions from the manager and in the best interests of the beneficial owners, the unit holders. The price of a unit is determined according to regulations and is based on the value of the assets and the number of units in existence.

Common investment funds are special kinds of collective investment schemes that are established as a trust and a charity. Investment in these is restricted to charities registered in England and Wales.

Investment trusts are not in fact trusts but limited liability companies with a board of directors who manage the company. The funds for an investment trust are contributed by shareholders and are invested in the shares of other companies. Investment trusts have a custodian as the registered holder of the fund's investments instead of a trustee. The investment management and administration is usually outsourced to a specialist fund management company. Shares in investment trusts are listed on a stock exchange and are subject to the same influences on their price as other companies' shares so they can trade at a premium or a discount to the value of the assets.

Open-ended investment companies (OEICs) are a relatively new form of collective investment scheme, which in essence combines the features of unit trusts and investment trusts. While they are a company like investment trusts, they are open-ended so that the capital of the company is variable. The assets of an OIEC are held by a depositary while a board of directors including an Authorized Corporate Director (ACD) responsible for principal operating matters manages the business. In many respects the ACD is similar to the unit trust manager and the depository, as they have responsibility for overseeing the ACD, not unlike the trustee. Shares in an OIEC can be listed on an exchange but most likely will be bought and sold via the ACD.

Private portfolios are diverse and very often this type of 'fund' is under the terminology of private banking although it can also be a fund set up under a family trust or as a result of a will. Few rules apply and the fund may be managed by an individual or by a manager. Many banks and brokers provide such facilities for high net worth clients in their asset management services.

An ***offshore fund*** denotes a collective investment scheme established outside the UK, usually open-ended companies issuing shares on a similar basis to a UK OEIC. Schemes established in the European Union are known as 'UCITS' (Undertakings for Collective Investment in Transferable Securities). They are eligible to be marketed in the UK subject to their recognition by the Financial Services Authority and compliance with UK marketing rules. Similar funds established in 'designated territories' i.e. those with close links to the UK such as the Channel Islands, Isle of Man and the Bahamas, may also be recognized by the FSA.

Venture capital trusts are companies similar to investment trusts but often with tax concessions for investors. These include an investor being able to claim tax relief (at the lower rate) on investments and receiving dividends free of tax and certain capital gains tax relief. Certain restrictions apply to venture capital trusts in terms of holdings in companies and the size of individual investments made each year.

Funds can be *open-ended* and *closed-ended*. The difference between open-ended and closed-ended funds concerns the ability to continuously issue and redeem shares or units or whether there is a fixed amount of capital in issue. Unit trusts and OEICs are examples of open-ended funds, investment and venture capital trusts, closed-ended. (See Table 7.1.)

Table 7.1 Summary of the differences between unit trusts, OEICs and investment trusts

	Unit trusts	OEICs	Investment trusts
Status of investors	Share in collective rights of assets Access to independent trustee	Investors are shareholders Rights are laid down in the regulations	Investors are shareholders in the investment trust Rights laid down in the Companies Acts
Open/closed ended	Open-ended Units in existence rise or fall dependent on investors	Open-ended Can redeem or issue shares on demand of investors	Closed-ended Fixed capital which can only be varied with permission of shareholders
Buying/selling	Normally bought and sold through managers Bid/offer spread of approx. 5% Can be single price	Bought or sold through Authorized Corporate Director (ACD) Single price but ACD may require payment of dilution levy	After launch they are bought and sold through brokers for a commission payment in the secondary market Price fixed by market
Price	Directly related to value of underlying portfolio and charges as laid down by regulator	Single price dependent on valuation of assets within fund	Dependent on market demand Shares usually traded at a discount to net asset value
Securities within the trust/company	90% of portfolio must be held in authorized/eligible stock markets	Invest in portfolio of shares and other securities	Wide range of securities can be purchased including unquoted and emerging market shares
Borrowing powers	Temporary, no longer than 3 months	Subject to any restrictions in instrument of incorporation No more than 10% of scheme property can be borrowed on any one day	Agreed in company's articles and may be increased by sanction of members
Management	Manager of trust with authority of trustee	ACD must be a corporation to provide for continuity	At least two directors
Meetings for investors	No requirement for regular meetings	Annual general meeting Other meetings at directors' calling	Annual general meeting and as required under Companies Acts

Source: DMS Ltd.

Managing funds, particularly when it is for a substantial value and for many participants is a complex business, which also has significant costs attached to it. There are also many regulations, rules and directives that must be adhered to. The basic reason for the funds being managed is, as we have already stated, to provide capital growth and/or income. Given the statement above it is no surprise that many fund management companies are the large investment banks and insurance companies, with smaller funds being managed by stockbrokers and specialist investment houses. If the fund is constituted as a trust, the manager and the trustee are the key people as they are parties to the deed which establishes the fund. What are the manager and the trustee actually responsible for?

In general terms, the manager is responsible for:

- Investment decisions
- Marketing
- Operations

The trustee is responsible for:

- Safeguarding the investments
- Maintaining the register of holders
- Collecting and distributing income
- Looking after the interests of holders

If the fund is constituted as a company its directors will operate it with the assets being held by a custodian or depositary. Functions, but not responsibilities, can be delegated to other parties such as specialist investment management, administration, registration and safe-custody providers. Naturally each fund will appoint auditors and/or reporting accountants. Of obvious interest to the investor and therefore to the managers of funds is the performance of the fund. As we have already noted, this interest is not confined to whether the fund has met its objectives but also to how it has performed in comparison to other similar funds and also to other types of investment vehicles. As a result, in their marketing fund managers will often make a comparison on performance, for example against the return on an equivalent investment in, say, a building society account. However, the investor needs to consider the background to the figures and how investment returns will perform under different economic environments as well as different risk situations.

Over a longer term, say, 10 or 15 years, a diversified equity-based investment will provide a higher return than a deposit-based savings account, not least because a successful manager will nurture the capital in the equity-based fund whereas the deposit-based fund is increased only by the addition of interest over the same period. It therefore follows that only in a sustained period of high interest would a deposit-based account outperform an equity-based fund. The risk inherent in the deposit-based savings account is less than in the equity-based investment (although the use of derivatives has reduced the impact of market 'crashes' on the performance of equity-based funds).

We also need to be aware of the government's and regulators' concern that investors should neither receive misleading data nor be pressurized into buying an investment. One key way in which this is achieved is by requiring investors to have the right to a cooling-off period or the right-to-cancel period when they can reverse their initial instructions having had a period to reflect on their decision. One solution to the need for supplying valuations and other data to investors, trustees and regulators is to utilize the services of companies that offer Fund Administration.

The duties and responsibilities of the fund manager and the trustees or custodian/depositary are clearly defined in the regulations and require the two roles to be quite separate and independent of each other. This separation of the prime functions of investment decisions from custody of the investments is a basic element of investor protection. While the delegation restrictions prevent, say, a fund manager appointing its trustee as the investment manager, it allows a fund to appoint a specialist administration company to carry out all tasks except investment management. These appointments, or outsourcing, are becoming more common in order to keep costs reasonable but they need to be supported by comprehensive and precise agreements known as 'service level agreements' (SLAs).

Another area that is important in fund management is portfolio accounting and controls. This is an important aspect of fund management and fund administration because the accurate and complete record of transactions carried in the fund, expenses incurred and income into the fund is quite obviously of fundamental importance. What is required? Managers must:

- Maintain investment accounts that separate capital transactions from income transactions
- Provide statements of gains and losses, realized and unrealized
- Show holdings in the portfolio and movement in the holdings
- Show cash coming in to and out of the fund
- Give current and comparative positions and valuations
- Provide various analyses and projections to enable tracking and adjustment to the portfolio to maintain performance in relation to yield and income distribution targets

Other important issues are the compliance with the fund's investment objectives and policies as set out in the trust deed, scheme of particulars or other documents related to the fund such as a prospectus. Compliance will include any limits on the fund set out in the documents or in the regulation applying to the fund. Various limits will apply such as:

- Percentage of the funds value that can be invested in the securities of a single issuer
- Percentage of the funds value that can be held in unlisted securities
- Liquidity in the assets to be held
- Use of derivatives

- Efficient portfolio management (EPM) rationales
- Approved markets

Accounting controls will include regular reconciliations of cash, dividend and interest records and stock positions with banks and trustees for both the capital and income account. These will be the subject of compliance monitoring and the annual audit. Realized and unrealized profit and loss and income is also an important issue. Transactions in the portfolio lead to realized and unrealized profits and losses. In this case transactions refer to the purchase and sale of assets, which may be closed off against an existing position to generate a realized profit or loss or be held as positions in the portfolio generating unrealized profit or loss. Other transactions might be in foreign securities or cash and these will produce gains or losses when converted to the base currency of the fund. Likewise, income collection relating to dividends and interest on cash held together with any fees or commissions earned is a function of fund administration and detailed records must be kept. Paying expenses, charges and taxes is also part of the function while another aspect, taxation issues, which will vary from fund to fund and by jurisdiction, must be addressed

We considered earlier in the book the importance of pricing for traders but equally important for investors and fund managers is the pricing and valuation of investments and investment products. Where a fund is open-ended and therefore continuously issuing and redeeming shares or units, regular valuations are essential. However, it is also a requirement for any type of fund to carry out these regular valuations to determine the basis for amount attributable to each participant. The value of a fund depends on the value of the assets held in the fund and is referred to as the net asset value or NAV. Regulations will determine the way and how often the manager must perform a valuation. The majority of funds are valued daily or weekly and the prospectus or scheme particulars will stipulate the valuation days and the time at which the valuation is carried out, called the valuation point.

Fund valuation consists of a series of steps:

1 Value the shares held in each security at the market price
2 Aggregate the values of the securities
3 Add the amount of uninvested cash held in the fund
4 Add income received/receivable
5 Deduct expenses etc. including provisions

The totals of steps 2 and 3 provide the portfolio or capital value and adding steps 4 and 5 gives the net asset value.

Shares and units are generally traded at a single price, but for unit trusts, regulations require the calculation of different prices, in this case

- **Creation price** the price based on the market-dealing offer prices of the underlying holdings and payable to the trustee for the creation of new units
- **Cancellation price** the price based on the market-dealing bid prices of the underlying holdings and payable by the trustee on the cancellation of the units
- **Buying price** the price paid by investors for units (usually includes the managers' initial charge)
- **Selling price** the price paid by the manager to investors selling their units which is less than the buying price but not less than the cancellation price

Accurate valuations and pricing are critical in ensuring that no investor is disadvantaged or treated unequally. Controls and checks are used to prevent errors in valuations and pricing but nevertheless any that occur must be reported to the trustee. Any error greater than $\frac{1}{2}$% may result in compensation being paid by the manager under the regulations.

Interestingly, managers are managing a fund in the style of the individual manager, the fund management company's style or the style of the fund. Hence we have terms such as 'active' and 'passive' management, as well as 'top-down' and 'bottom-up' styles. A top-down style is where the manager first looks at the economic analysis to identify prospering or soon to be prospering national or regional economies followed by identifying industries or areas of business activity that will benefit. Finally the manager identifies the individual companies that will or should, as a result, enjoy profitable growth. Bottom-up requires managers to seek out well-managed companies and then to analyse the current performance and prospects for these companies before deciding on whether to invest. Passive managers rarely change the composition of the portfolio other than pre-determined changes in funds such as 'tracker funds' that mirror an index and where changes to the portfolio follow changes to the constituent shares in the index.

In contrast, active managers regularly change the composition of the assets of the fund in response to changes or anticipated changes in the international and national economic environment and also changes or expected changes in the performance of individual companies, markets or market sectors.

Active management does not mean 'trading' and the activity will be monitored to make sure that the costs are not outweighing the benefits of active management. Passive funds can be 'adjusted' so that the fund tracks an index but not to the same weightings, being more heavily weighted to certain stocks. This is known as 'tilting' the fund.

Many things affect the performance of funds, not least the limits imposed on holdings in stocks and yet the manager must attempt to reduce risks through diversification. The combination of the diversification and limits may actually reduce the upside potential of the fund. The performance of individual managers varies as stock selection, weightings, etc. affect the performance of the fund over the short, medium and longer term. The competency of the manager, charges and integrity all matter as does the investment skill and the quality of information used to make decisions. Foreign exchange rates, interest rates, sudden changes in economic growth, 'market crashes' can all adversely affect the fund in the short term. An incorrect view can be just as damaging, which was discovered by a fund manager in the 1990s when their not unreasonable assumption that the FTSE index had peaked resulted in them selling stocks and placing the funds on deposit. The index kept on rising so the performance of the funds was poor in relative terms to other funds.

To mitigate against such eventualities, the fund manager will, where permitted by the trustees and mandates, use derivatives to hedge the risks. Derivatives can also be used for asset-allocation purposes to enable immediate switching of exposures between asset classes. This was illustrated in Chapter 4.

Portfolio weightings and profiles are how a manager will decide, within the limits and conditions applied to the fund, the markets and categories of stocks and assets to be used. There will be considerations, depending on the style, on the weighting of the assets in the portfolio by country, sector, etc. A top-down manager will have an asset allocation model, a bottom-up manager a model portfolio. This establishes the weightings and the manager may then be in line, overweight or underweight. This may be deliberate or because of changes to the markets, economies or stocks.

Managers may be fully invested, i.e. all the investor's funds have been invested in assets. In general terms a fund is better off fully invested, but this is not without problems for the manager. First, a fund using derivatives must have a certain amount of cash available to meet margin calls and second, a successful open-ended fund attracting cash may mean the manager is faced with difficulties such as limits being reached or investment being diversified further with a resulting increase in risk. When a manager decides to change the asset allocation in the portfolio they are also aware that they may adversely affect the shares prices of the assets particularly in smaller, less liquid companies.

The profile of the fund is determined by the objectives. A high-income fund will have the majority of its assets as high-yielding stocks or fixed-interest securities while growth funds seek out companies with good prospects and reinvest the income into those companies, generating capital growth. Balanced funds seek to achieve the best of both with reasonable growth and level of income. Larger funds such as life funds will tend to subdivide the total fund into subfunds with a different emphasis and in order to have funds available for corporate actions or new issues a manager may decide to be tactically liquid, i.e. not fully invested.

Management style has its contrasts, as we can see from looking at chartists and quants. Chartists are managers who rely on their interpretation of graphs and extrapolation into the future to guide their investment decisions. Quants, on the other hand, engage in detailed quantitative analysis of fundamental data and look for numerical absolutes and trends to suggest or support investment decisions. Both have merit as do programme trades which are activated when the computer system detects that certain preset conditions prevail, i.e. large movements up or down in individual markets or sectors or limit trades that are activated when individual shares hit certain prices or price conditions.

Obviously the quality and timing of information is crucial and will cover everything from data on the company and market data to directors' dealings and political situations. Volume of business and market share, return on capital employed (ROCE) and market capitalization, price earnings ratios, dividend yields, etc. are all key elements of information needed by managers.

Operations teams support the fund management activity through portfolio administration functions. Managers deal via brokers in the assets to be held in the portfolio and deals on a best execution basis. Once dealt, the transaction is settled via the settlement convention applicable and registration is effected into or out of the fund's name, i.e. the trustee or custodian/depositary must be advised as they are the legal owners. Efficient portfolio administration must deal with issues such as the purchase or sale of stock where a corporate action such as a dividend payment must be claimed or paid. Assets of a fund may be held in a nominee at a custodian or correspondent bank where they will be clearly designated. Important records must be maintained for the funds to meet regulatory requirements and will require the manager to produce evidence that:

- allocation of any bulk trades between different funds was fair
- the securities and amounts are clearly identified
- the trade has been executed promptly and in a timely manner
- the reason for the trade
- that the price obtained constituted best execution

This provides an audit trail showing rationale and efficiency from strategy inception to settlement. Operations teams need to be aware of the fund management style, objectives and trust requirements. They must be able to accurately price the assets in the fund and obtain the managers' sign-off on those prices. Income, benefits and accounting records are all fundamental support functions, so too is client reporting.

We have already noted that a comparison is made between different types of investment products and between funds, often allied to marketing. Many industry journals offer tables of performance enabling an element of measurement to take place but it is important to view comparisons objectively, as simple performance data between two funds does not tell the whole story. Types of retail funds are categorized by the FSA into categories of collective investment schemes according to investment policy but these cannot solely be used to make comparison. Measuring income yield is one possible measure of performance.

Income yield can be defined as:

Income for year/investment cost × 100%

Using this formula historic distribution yield would utilize the income over the last 12 months, current yield would be over the current calendar year and the forecast or prospective yield would be the likely yield over the next 12 months. We might also be interested in the portfolio yield or internal rate of return. This represents expected future annual income to be generated by the portfolio expressed as a percentage of the current net asset value of the fund on a buying basis, thus:

Future annual income of current portfolio/cost of buying portfolio × 100%

Note: Different types of measures would apply to portfolios with a majority of the assets held in fixed dated stocks or securities.

Total return = capital growth + income for period/cost/value at beginning of period × 100%

If we looked at two funds that started with a value of £1000 and £2000 respectively at the beginning of the period and had a value of £2000 and £4000 respectively at the end then on the face of it each has performed the same, i.e. increased the value by 100%. However, if the second fund had received an inflow of £1000 the figures would change such that the adjusted return would be 50% if the inflow occurred at the end of the period or 33% if it had occurred at the beginning.

Performance measurement can be made to benchmarks such as the FTSE 100 or All Share index. Thus a geographic spread of assets can be benchmarked so that trustees of a pension fund, for instance, might require assets to be invested in the USA, the UK and Japan and the benchmark is to be the S&P 500, FTSE 100 and Nikkei 225 indices. If the benchmark calculation of the movement in these indices was, for instance, 14.5% and the fund's total return was calculated as 20% it has comfortably outperformed the benchmark.

Fund managers often change the asset allocation if new funds are received and the trustees need to know how much the change to the asset allocation has increased the risk to the portfolio to achieve the return. A common method is to look at volatility of the portfolio relative to the index and this is measured by reference to standard deviation, i.e. how far the individual returns deviate from their average value. As the standard deviation of an index can be calculated by taking a series of readings at intervals, this can be compared with the standard deviation of the portfolio values taken for the same intervals. The comparison will show whether the portfolio is more or less risky than the index.

Clearly the maintenance of accurate records of assets held, bought, sold and income and pricing, etc. is crucial and operations teams need to be very much aware of why this is the case.

Today there are many different ways in which people can save, protect themselves and their property and seek to increase both their income and capital. Individuals and groups of individuals have participated in the buying of stocks and shares for many centuries. Examples of the concept of investing in an idea or scheme with a view to making a gain in both income and capital would be people who purchased shares or bonds in the canal and railway companies as they pioneered their businesses in the nineteenth century. Others invested in the projects being masterminded by the Victorians in farflung corners of the empire. Some made their fortunes, others lost everything. Investors in the USA suffered similar rollercoaster experiences as the relentless surge in share buying pushed prices, and fortunes, ever higher, until the 'crash' in the 1920s. History is littered with highs and lows, profits and losses, 'black' Monday, Wednesday and Fridays, the collapse of Enron, etc. All have something in common. It is the impact on the small investor through the impact on the holdings in funds and other retail products.

Today there is still uncertainty surrounding investment decisions but there are many diverse products that are available to investors that allow a greater degree of control over the 'risk' that they take as well as affording them a better chance to see their investments and savings grow through greater diversification. These retail products, as they are known, are available in many forms, varying from established vehicles such as pensions and life assurance to newer products based on venture capital and offshore 'tax-efficient' trusts.

Within each product grouping there is usually a wide diversity of products and schemes to suit all tastes. This can be illustrated by the numerous 'green' funds that will not invest in environmentally unfriendly companies as well as the 'Islamic' funds that avoid companies that are in conflict with the Koran. In the UK unit trusts have proved a popular form of investment while government privatizations of nationalized industries such as British Telecommunications expanded the concept of share ownership to parts of the population that had never before invested in shares in companies. Retail products can be specialist or multiple investments based and there are numerous innovative products available to the public.

The government offers many of these products and, through tax advantages, encourages others. Examples are National Savings, including Premium Bonds and government bonds (Gilts). Companies offer products and charge fees for managing the amounts paid in by investors, often providing either spectacular gain, far and above the 'average' investment products, or end up providing nothing. One example is hedge funds. The choice of retail products available is enormous and investors are therefore faced with a challenge to identify those products that are suitable and those that will provide the best returns. Emerging market funds may not be ideal for retirement planning but ISAs could be. On the other hand, emerging market funds offer the possibility of significant gains. There is, thankfully, considerable information about the various products readily available and independent financial advisors offer their services to make sure that all the possible options are covered before the decision is taken. The source of investment products in terms of both issuance and selling is also diverse.

Retail products are a significant part of today's financial markets. The generation of wealth has created the need for investment vehicles that satisfy not just the income potential but also capital growth, tax efficiency, life insurance and pension provisions. Allied to this are products designed to provide everything from a means to pay off mortgages to settling school fees. Each of these products will have certain characteristics. The structure and return on the product is geared to the investors' requirements so that products have different risk and reward profiles. The source of products is enormous ranging from stock exchanges where company shares are listed and available for trading to life companies providing products with both an insurance and investment element to the product. The kind of terminology we see reflects this so we have expressions in every day use such as:

- With profits policies
- Endowment policies
- Guaranteed
- Fixed return

The sheer diversity of products makes detailed coverage of all of them beyond the scope of this book. However, we have looked at some of the key products associated with the retail markets and others are mentioned at various points in the book. Underlying all the vast business in funds and retail products is the capital markets and the products issued and traded there in the wholesale market. We must not forget here that there is a large industry of retail products offered by banks and building societies such as mortgages, current and deposit accounts, credit cards, loans and tax-efficient offshore investment schemes, etc., and these, together with the investment retail products, make a significant contribution to the merry-go-round of money in the wholesale and retail markets in the financial services industry.

Chapter 8

Changes and developments

The financial markets never stand still. Since the early days of organized trading, progress has been made in all aspects of the markets including, of course, the trading itself. In the early days most exchanges were commodities based, then as the financial markets developed so we had stock exchanges and later, derivatives exchanges. Today there are exchanges which trade many different products reflecting the sophistication of the end-users. The globalization of the financial services industry and the consequent rationalization has created a situation where the major international banks are members of most of the main exchanges. It is hardly surprising, then, that the drive towards mergers of the exchanges is coming from the large member firms who have most to gain from operating on a few mega-exchanges rather than a host of exchanges located along geographical and country lines. Pressure on the traditional exchanges is coming also from the Internet-based exchanges. Cross-border trading has never been easier, although it is not always as cheap as it should be.

Let us look at the type of changes that have taken place, are taking place now and will take place in the future. We can start with Europe and Scandinavia.

The introduction of the euro and the notional Eurozone inevitably led to the key participants in the European markets focusing on what change would be needed and how it might come about. Monetary union removed a vast amount of hitherto foreign exchange dealing and, of course, created a European Central Bank. Elsewhere the international central securities depositories of Cedel Bank and Euroclear were looking at settlement and, realizing that a Eurozone scenario would need a Eurozone depository, both put forward suggestions for the merging, linking and absorbing of domestic CSDs.

Of course, this aim was somewhat dependent on the mergers, alliances and links that might happen at exchange and clearing house level. The dominant exchanges at the time were the London Stock Exchange, Deutsche Borse, EUREX (the German derivatives exchange) and LIFFE. There were also the Paris Bourse and derivatives markets, MATIF and MONEP. In Scandinavia the Swedish OM Groupen had established a market not only in Stockholm but also in London, the London Securities and Derivatives Exchange (OMLX). More importantly it was selling its systems to other markets.

By the end of 2001 things looked very different. Cedel Bank had become Clearstream, an organization 50% owned by Deutsche Borse. The securities markets of Paris, Brussels and Amsterdam had announced that they would merge into an entity to be called Euronext and that the clearing house would be Clearnet. Meanwhile in the UK LIFFE had moved forward from its low point and the London Stock Exchange, having aborted its merger talks with Deutsche Borse following an unsuccessful bid from OM, was, along with Deutsche Borse and Euronext, invited to bid for LIFFE. Euronext won the day and also announced that the Portuguese exchange would also be joining the grouping, thus it began to look the likely winner in the race to be the 'pan-European' exchange.

Markets have appeared like JIWAY, BrokerTech and virt X (created by the merger of the former Tradepoint Stock Exchange and the Swiss Exchange), in addition to various exchanges around the world trading electricity and weather products and the Cantor Index for those who enjoy spread betting. Euronext introduced the first wine futures and the London Stock Exchange introduced TechMark for the listing of technology stocks.

On the clearing front, the London Clearing House had linked with CREST to provide a central clearing counterparty facility for equity trades made on SETS. It had also successfully launched its Repoclear and Swapclear products and had been in discussions with Clearnet about links.

As 2002 started, NASDAQ was still keen to get a toehold in Europe and eyes were looking towards the LSE to see what course of action they would take following their failure to get LIFFE. In the USA and Canada there has been change that only a few years ago would have seemed unlikely, for instance T + 1 settlement for equity securities by 2005 is an objective and the Chicago derivatives exchanges, for so long fiercely independent and autonomous, have been spurred on by the link between NASDAQ and LIFFE to offer the same products, joined together to create One Chicago for trading single-stock futures contracts.

In the Asia–Pacific region we have mentioned earlier how stock and derivatives exchanges in Hong Kong and Singapore have joined together and while a 'single Asian currency' may be some way off other changes will undoubtedly occur in response to the changes elsewhere.

On the product front there was plenty of change taking place too. Apart from the growing number of pan-European indices, the market in Exchange Traded Funds had also shown a significant growth. Elsewhere in the retail markets Individual Savings Accounts (ISAs) had replaced Personal Equity Plans (PEPs) and although initially there was strong growth in sales, the slide in equity markets, the fear of a global recession and the aftermath of the 11 September atrocities led observers to predict that the sales of ISAs before the end of the tax year would be lower than in previous years. Credit derivatives had also seen growth in use through the late 1990s and into the 2000s. The collapse of Enron, for the time being reportedly the largest ever corporate collapse, would make many operators in these products aware of their exposure to these types of derivatives and, although not quite the same, it was likely to be a rerun of the problems Lloyd's names experienced as the impact of insurance that had to be paid out became apparent. Indeed some observers predicted that problems and issues like liquidity in the predominantly OTC market for credit derivatives would lead to products being developed for trading on exchanges where the counterparty risk was with a clearing house.

In fund management the changes have been in the form of rationalization as fund managers merge or are taken over, regulatory changes, opportunities in Eurozone products and the expanding use of diverse products in funds. This is perhaps illustrated by the decision of M&G to include a hedge fund in the life portfolio which shows not only the sophistication of fund management companies but also, in some cases, the acceptance of hedge funds as suitable assets for their portfolios.

All these changes impacted or are going to impact to a greater or lesser extent on the operations functions. The move towards a consolidated European market and clearing structure will speed up the move towards true STP and T + 1 and trade day settlement. Margined settlement of securities and derivatives through central clearing counterparties will put greater pressure on disciplined settlement, systems, use of collateral, innovative and quality client service and management of operational risk. In turn this will require retraining of personnel, revamped procedures and controls.

Globalization is already extensive with global banks and global funds and yet there are still many areas of the 'financial world', which will become more globalized in the years to come. There are still emerging markets with enormous potential for investors and service providers and investors, benefiting from growth in earnings and wealth in many parts of the world seeking ever more attractive places to put their funds. Industry and commerce seek more advantageous ways to raise capital and maximize profits. In response the banks and brokers and fund managers develop the products to service this demand, the growth in asset-backed securities and securitization being an example.

New products mean new operational requirements and, in particular, system capability to generate not only the management of risk but also the capacity to handle this new business. Sadly we must also reflect on the issue of crime and terrorism and how this impacts on the industry as a whole, the organizations and the individuals working within it. Constant vigilance, comprehensive security against hackers, money launderers, fraudsters and criminals costs billions of dollars. Today disaster-recovery requirements are significant even for the smallest organization and, coupled with the changes in the structures or clearing, custody and settlement and the regulatory change, which will always be there, it really does present a massive challenge to operations managers and supervisors.

Developing and documenting procedures and the maintenance of those procedures becomes vital. Comprehending and then complying with the global regulation and local practices demands comprehensive knowledge, tact, quality supporting staff and systems and above all first-class communication. The markets are changing rapidly as are the skill sets and roles within operations and the managers need to respond to this.

Appendix 1

ISSA 2000 recommendations

The ISSA recommendations 2000 are:

1 Securities systems have a primary responsibility to their users and other stakeholders. They must provide effective low-cost processing. Services should be priced equitably.
2 Securities systems must allow the option of network access on an interactive basis. They should cope with peak capacity without any services degradation, and have sufficient standby capabilities to recover operations in a reasonably short period within each processing day.
3 The industry worldwide must satisfy the need for efficient, fast settlement by full adherence to the International Securities Numbering process (ISO 6166) and uniform usage of ISO 15022 standards for all securities messages. The industry should seek to introduce a global client and counterpart identification methodology (BIC–ISO 9362) to further facilitate straightthrough processing. Applications and programmes should be structured in such a way as to facilitate open interaction between all parties.
4 Each market must have clear rules assuring investor protection by safeguarding participants from the financial risks of failed settlement and ensuring that listed companies are required to follow sound policies on corporate governance, transfer of economic benefits and shareholder rights.

5 The major risks in securities systems should be mitigated by five key measures, namely;
   - The implementation of real delivery versus payment
   - The adoption of a trade date plus one settlement cycle in a form that does not increase operational risk
   - The minimization of funding and liquidity constraints by enabling stock lending and borrowing, broad-based cross-collateralization, the use of repos and netting as appropriate
   - The enforcement of scripless settlement
   - The establishment of mandatory trade matching and settlement performance measures.

6 Convergence of securities systems, both within countries and across borders, should be encouraged where this eliminates operational risk, reduces cost and enhances market efficiency.

7 Investor compliance with the laws and regulations in the home countries of their investments should be part of their regulators' due diligence process. Investors, in turn, should be treated equitably in the home country of their investments, especially in respect to their rights to shareholder benefits and concessionary arrangements under double-tax agreements.

8 Local laws and regulations should ensure that there is segregation of client assets from the principal assets of their custodian; and no possible claim on client assets in the event of custodian bankruptcy or a similar event. Regulators and markets, to further improve investor protection, should work
   - To ensure clarity on the applicable law on cross-border transactions
   - To seek international agreement on a legally enforceable definition of finality in a securities transaction
   - To ensure that local law fully protects the rights of beneficial owners
   - To strengthen securities laws both to secure the rights of the pledgee and the protection accorded to client assets held in securities systems.

Source: ISSA 2000.

Appendix 2

G30 recommendations

1 All comparisons of trades between direct market participants (i.e. brokers, broker dealers and other exchange members) should be accomplished by T + 0. Matched trade details should be linked to the settlement system.

2 Indirect market participants (such as institutional investors, and other indirect trading counterparties) should achieve positive affirmation of trade details on T + 1.

3 Each country should have in place an effective and fully developed central securities depository, organized and managed to encourage the broadest possible direct and indirect industry participation. The range of depository-eligible instruments should be as wide as possible. Immobilization or dematerialization of financial instruments should be achieved to the utmost extent possible.

4 Each market is encouraged to reduce settlement risk by introducing either Real Time Gross Settlement or a trade netting system that fully meets the 'Lamfalussy Recommendations'.

5 Delivery versus payment (DVP) should be employed as the method for settling all securities transactions. DVP is defined as follows: simultaneous, irrevocable and immediately available exchange of securities and cash on a continuous basis throughout the day.

6 Payments associated with the settlement of securities transactions and the servicing of securities portfolios should be made consistent across all instruments and markets by adopting the 'same-day' funds convention.

7 A rolling settlement system should be adopted by all markets. Final settlement for all trades should occur no later than T + 3.
8 Securities lending and borrowing should be encouraged as a method of expediting the settlement of securities transactions. Existing regulatory and taxation barriers that inhibit the practice of lending securities should be removed.
9 Each country should adopt the standard for securities messages developed by the International Organization of Standardization (ISO Standard 7775). In particular, countries should adopt the ISIN numbering system for securities issues as defined in the ISO Standard 6166.

Source: Clearance & Settlement Systems in the World's Securities Markets, G30 (1989) and updated by ISSA (May 1995).

Appendix 3

Global derivatives exchanges

Australia	
ASX – Australian Stock Exchange	www.asx.com.au
SFE – Sydney Futures Exchange	www.sfe.com.au
Belgium	
Brussels Exchanges	www.bxs.be
Brazil	
BM&F – Bolsa De Mercadorias and Futuros	www.bmf.com.br
Sao Paulo Stock Exchange	www.bvrj.com.br
Canada	
ME – Montreal Exchange	www.me.org
TFE – Toronto Futures Exchange	www.tse.com
VSE – Vancouver Stock Exchange	www.vse.ca
WCE – Winnipeg Commodity Exchange	www.wce.ca
China	
SME – Shanghai Metal Exchange	www.shme.com
Denmark	
FUTOP – Guarantee Fund for Danish Futures and Options	www.xcse.dk
Finland	
FOEX – The Finnish Options Exchange	www.foex.fi
SOM – Finnish Securities and Derivatives Exchange	www.som.fi

France

MATIF – Marche à Terme International de France	www.matif.fr
MONEP – Marche Des Options Negotiables De Paris	www.monep.fr

Germany

Hannover Commodity Exchange	www.wtb-hannover.de
Eurex	www.eurexchange.com

Hong Kong

HKEX – Hong Kong Exchanges & Clearing Ltd	www.hkex.com.hk

Hungary

BCE – Budapest Commodity Exchange	www.bce-bat.com
BSE – Budapest Stock Exchange	www.bse.hu

Israel

Tel Aviv Stock Exchange	www.tase.co.il

India

National Stock Exchange of India	www.nseindia.com

Italy

IDEM – Italian Derivatives Market	www.idem.it

Japan

Hanmon Commodity Exchange	www.hce.or.jp
OSE – Osaka Securities Exchange	quote.ose.or.jp (not www.)
TCE – Tokyo Commodity Exchange	www.tocom.or.jp
TGE – Tokyo Grain Exchange	www.tge.or.jp
TIFFE – Tokyo International Financial Futures Exchange	www.tiffe.or.jp
TSE – Tokyo Stock Exchange	www.tse.or.jp

Korea

Korea Stock Exchange	www.kse.or.kr

Malaysia

KLCE – Kuala Lumpur Commodity Exchange	www.klce.com.my
Commodity and Monetary Exchange of Malaysia	commex.com.my

Netherlands

EURONEXT	www.euronext.com

New Zealand

NZFOE – New Zealand Futures & Options Exchange	www.sfe.com.au

Norway

Olso Stock Exchange	www.ose.no/english/

Portugal

BDP – Bolsa De Derivados De Porto	www.bdp.pt

Russia

The Russian Exchange	www.re.ru

Singapore

Singapore Commodity Exchange	www.sicom.com.sg
Singapore Exchange	www.sgx.com

South Africa

SAFEX – South African Futures Exchange	www.safex.co.za
JSE – Johannesburg Stock Exchange	www.jse.co.za

Spain

MEFF	www.meff.es

Sweden

OM Stockholmbörsen	www.stockholmborsen.se

Switzerland

EUREX	www.eurexchange.com

Turkey

Istanbul Stock Exchange	www.ise.org

United Kingdom

IPE – International Petroleum Exchange	www.ipe.uk.com
LIFFE – London International Financial Futures & Options Exchange	www.liffe.com
LME – London Metal Exchange	www.lme.co.uk
OMLX – The London Securities & Derivatives Exchange	www.stockholmborsen.se

United States of America

AMEX – American Stock Exchange	www.amex.com
CBOE – Chicago Board Options Exchange	www.cboe.com
CBOT – Chicago Board of Trade	www.cbot.com
CME – Chicago Mercantile Exchange	www.cme.com
CSCE – Coffee, Sugar & Cocoa Exchange Inc.	www.csce.com
KCBT – Kansas City Board of Trade	www.kcbt.com
MGE – Minneapolis Grain Exchange	www.mgex.com
NYBOT – New York Board of Trade	www.nybot.com
NYCE – New York Cotton Exchange	www.nyce.com
NYMEX – New York Mercantile Exchange	www.nymex.com
NYSE – New York Stock Exchange	www.nyse.com
PHLX – Philadelphia Stock Exchange	www.phlx.com
NASDAQ	www.nasdaq.com

Glossary

30/360 Also 360/360 or 30(E)/360. A day/year count convention assuming 30 days in each calendar month and a 'year' of 360 days; adjusted in America for certain periods ending on the 31st day of the month (and then sometimes known as 30(A)/360).

360/360 Same as **30/360**.

AAA The highest credit rating for a company or asset – the risk of default is negligible.

Accreting swap A swap where the notional principal increases during the life of the swap.

Accrued interest Interest due on a bond or other fixed-income security that must be paid by the buyer of a security to its seller. Usual compensation: coupon rate of interest times elapsed days from prior interest payment date (i.e. coupon date) up to but not including settlement date.

ACT/360 A day/year count convention taking the number of calendar days in a period and a 'year' of 360 days.

ACT/365 Also ACT/365 Fixed or ACT/365-F. A day/year count convention taking the number of calendar days in a period and a 'year' of 365 days. Under the ISDA definitions used for interest rate swap documentation, ACT/365 means the same as ACT/ACT.

ACT/365 Fixed See **ACT/365**.

ACT/365-F See **ACT/365**.

ACT/ACT For an interest rate swap, a day/year count convention dividing the number of calendar days in the interest period that fall in a leap year by 366 and dividing the remainder by 365.

Actual settlement date Date the transaction effectively settles in the clearing house (exchange of securities eventually against cash).

Add-on In capital-adequacy calculations, the extra capital required to allow for the possibility of a deal moving into profit before a mark-to-market calculation is next made.

AEX Amsterdam Exchanges (now part of EURONEXT).

Affirmation Affirmation refers to the counterparty's agreement with the terms of the trade as communicated.

Agent One who executes orders for or otherwise acts on behalf of another (the principal) and is subject to its control and authority. The agent takes no financial risk and may receive a fee or commission.

Agent bank A commercial bank that provides services as per their instructions.

Agreement among (by) underwriters A legal document forming underwriting banks into a syndicate for a new issue and giving the lead manager the authority to act on behalf of the group. In the 'among' form, a direct legal relationship links each underwriter to every other underwriter. In the 'by' form the legal relationship is established between the managers and the individual underwriter. However, the agreement also serves to define relationships between underwriters.

All or none (AON) Instruction to buy or sell the entire order in a single transaction, i.e. not to execute a partial transaction. AON restricts the size but not necessarily the time of the transaction.

Allocation (Give Up) The process of moving the trade from the executing broker to the clearing broker in exchange-traded derivatives.

Allotment The amount of a new issues (i.e. number of bonds) given to a syndicate member by the lead manager.

Alternative investment market (AIM) Second tier of market run by the London Stock Exchange.

American depository receipt (ADR) Document giving the owner rights to UK shares. They are effectively bearer documents.

American style option The holder of the long position can choose to exercise the position into the underlying instrument until the expiry day.

AMEX American Stock Exchange.

Amortization Accounting procedure that gradually reduces the cost value of a limited life asset or intangible asset through periodic charges to income. The purpose of amortization is to reflect the resale or redemption value. Amortization also refers to the reduction of debt by regular payments of interest and principal to pay off a loan by maturity.

Amortizing swap A swap where the notional principal decreases during the life of the swap.

AMS Dealing system for the Stock Exchange of Hong Kong (Automatic Order Matching and Execution System).

Announcement In a new bond issue, the day on which a release is sent to prospective syndicate members describing the offering and inviting underwriters and selling group members to join the syndicate.

Annual general meeting (AGM) Meeting of shareholders which a company must call every year. Its main purposes are to receive the accounts, vote on dividends and appoint directors.

Annuity For the recipient, an arrangement whereby the individual receives a prespecified payment annually for a prespecified number of years.

Arbitrageur A trader who takes advantage of profitable opportunities arising from price anomalies.

As agent One who acts as an intermediary or broker in a transaction and who assumes no financial risk. For this service, the firm receives a stated commission or fee.

Asian option See **Average rate option**.

Ask price Price at which a market-maker will sell stock. Also known as the offer price.

ASSET Dealing system for the Stock Exchange of Thailand (Automated System of the Stock Exchange of Thailand).

Asset allocation The use of derivatives by a fund manager, to immediately gain or reduce exposure to different markets.

Asset-backed securities Debt obligations that pay principal and interest; principal only or interests only; deferred interest and negative interest using a combination of factors and rate multipliers. The issues are serviced by multiple vendors that supply the necessary data to make the corresponding payments.

Asset swap An interest rate swap or currency swap used to change the interest rate exposure and/or the currency exposure of an investment. Also used to describe the package of the swap plus the investment itself.

Assets Everything of value that is owned or is due: fixed assets (cash, buildings and machinery) and intangible assets (patents and goodwill).

Assignment The process by which the holder of a short option position is matched against a holder of a similar long option position who has exercised his right.

Association of British Insurers (ABI) A trade body of insurance companies through which they can air their views collectively on matters of common concern.

ASX Australian Stock Exchange.

At best order Type of order input into SETS which is completed against displayed orders at the best prices(s) available.

ATM See **At-the-money**.

At-the-money An option whose exercise price is equal, or very close to, the current market price of the underlying share. This option has no intrinsic value.

Auction Method by which the Bank of England issues gilts. Successful applicants pay the price that they offered.

Authentication agent A bank putting a signature on each physical bond to certify its genuineness prior to the distribution of the definitive bonds on the market.

Authorization Status required by the Financial Services and Markets Act 2000 for any firm that wants to conduct investment business.

Authorized Corporate Director (ACD) Organization which undertakes the role of managing the funds in an OEIC.

Authorized unit trust Unit trust which meets the requirements of the Financial Services Authority to allow it to be freely marketable.

Average rate option An option where the settlement is based on the difference between the strike and the average price of the underlying over a predetermined period. Also known as Asian options.

Average strike option An option that pays the difference between the average rate of the underlying over the life of the option and the rate at expiry.

Back-to-back transaction See **Turnaround**.

Balance of payments The difference between the total value of imports and exports. If imports are higher there is a deficit and if exports are higher there is a surplus.

Ballot A random selection of applicants for a new issue of shares.

Bank – commercial Organization that takes deposits and makes loans.

Bank – merchant Organization that specializes in advising on takeovers and corporate finance activities.

Bank of England The UK's central bank which undertakes policy decided by the Treasury and determines interest rates.

Bankers' acceptance Short-term negotiable discount note, drawn on and accepted by banks which are obliged to pay the face value amount at maturity.

Bargain Another word for a transaction or deal. It does not imply that a particularly favourable price was obtained.

Barrier option Also trigger option, exploding option or extinguishing option. An option which is either cancelled or activated if the underlying price reaches a predetermined barrier or trigger level. See **Knock-out option; knock-in option**.

Base currency Currency chosen for reporting purposes.

Basis (gross) The difference between the relevant cash instrument price and the futures price. Often used in the context of hedging the cash instrument.

Basis (value or net) The difference between the gross basis and the carry.

Basis point (B.P.) A change in the interest rate of one hundredth of one per cent (0.01%). One basis point is written as 0.01 when 1.0 represents 1%.

Basis risk The risk that the price or rate of one instrument or position might not move exactly in line with the price or rate of another instrument or position which is being used to hedge it.

Basis swap An interest rate swap where the interest payments that are exchanged between each party are different types of floating rates.

BBA British Bankers' Association.

Bear Investor who believes prices will fall.

Bearer document Documents which state on them that the person in physical possession (the bearer) is the owner.

Benchmark bond The most recently issued and most liquid government bond.

Beneficial owner The underlying owner of a security who has paid for the stock and is entitled to the benefits of ownership.

Bermudan option An option where the holder can choose to exercise on any of a series of pre-determined dates between the purchase of the option and expiry. See **American style option; European style option**.

Bid (a) The price or yield at which a purchaser is willing to buy a given security. (b) To quote a price or yield at which a purchaser is able to buy a given security.

BIFFEX The Baltic International Freight Futures Exchange.

Bilateral netting A netting system in which all trades executed on the same date in the same security between the same counterparties are grouped and netted to one final delivery versus payment.

Bill of exchange A money market instrument.

BIS Bank for International Settlements.

Blanket bond insurance Blanket insurance covering the transactions of all employees, officers and partners of an organization that protects against misplacement fraud and cheque forgery. Such coverage is required by the NYSE Constitution.

Block trade A purchase or sale of a large number of shares or dollar value of bonds normally much more than what constitutes a round lot in the market in question.

BMV-SENTRA Equity dealing system for the Mexican Stock Exchange.

BOLT Trading system of the Bombay Stock Exchange (Bombay Stock Exchange OnLine Trading).

Bond A certificate of debt, generally long-term, under the terms of which an issuer contracts, *inter alia*, to pay the holder a fixed principal amount on a stated future date and, usually, a series of interest payments during its life.

Bonus issue A free issue of shares to a company's existing shareholders. No money changes hands and the share price falls pro rata. It is a cosmetic exercise to make the shares more marketable. Also known as a capitalization or scrip issue.

Book entry transfer System of recording ownership of securities by computer where the owners do not receive a certificate. Records are kept (and altered) centrally in 'the book'.

Books closed day Last date for the registration of shares or bonds for the payment of the next.

Borrower's option See **Interest Rate Guarantee**.

BOVESPA São Paulo Stock Exchange.

Break A term used for any out-of-balance condition. A money break means that debits and credits are not equal. A trade break means that some information such as that from a contra broker is missing to complete that trade.

Bretton Woods Agreement An agreement that set a system of exchange rate stability after the Second World War, with all member currencies having a par value pegged to the US$, allowing a 1% variance. This was agreed by major economists from 44 countries. The International Monetary Fund and the World Bank were agreed to be set up at this conference.

Broken date A maturity date other than the standard ones normally quoted.

Broken period A period other than the standard ones normally quoted.

Broker/dealer Any member firm of the Stock Exchange except the specialists which are GEMMs and IDBs.

Broking The activity of representing a client as agent and charging commission for doing so.
Bull Investor who believes prices will rise.
Buying in The action taken by a broker failing to receive delivery of securities from a counterparty on settlement date to purchase these securities in the open market.
CAC 40 French Equity Index.
Caja de valores Depository/custodian for Argentinian shares.
Calendar spread The simultaneous purchase (or sale) of a futures or option contract for one date and the sale (or purchase) of a similar futures contract for a different date. See **Spread**.
Call deposits Deposits which can be called (or withdrawn) at the option of the lender (and in some cases the borrower) after a specified period. The period is short, usually one or two days, and interest is paid at prevailing short-term rates (call account).
Call option An option that gives the seller the right, but not the obligation, to buy a specified quantity of the underlying asset at a fixed price, on or before a specified date. The buyer of a call option has the obligation (because they have bought the right) to make delivery of the underlying asset if the option is exercised by the seller.
Call spread The purchase of a call option coupled with the sale of another call option at a different strike, expecting a limited rise or fall in the value of the underlying.
Callable bond A bond that the issuer has the right to redeem prior to maturity by paying some specified call price.
Cap Also ceiling. A package of interest rate options whereby, at each of a series of future fixing dates, if an agreed reference rate such as LIBOR is higher than the strike rate, the option buyer receives the difference between them, calculated on an agreed notional principal amount for the period until the next fixing date.
Capital adequacy Requirement for firms conducting investment business to have sufficient funds.
Capital gains tax (CGT) Tax payable by individuals on profit made on the disposal of assets.
Capital markets A term used to describe the means by which large amounts of money (capital) are raised by companies, govern-

ments and other organizations for long-term use and the subsequent trading of the instruments issued in recognition of such capital.

Capitalization issue See **Bonus issue**.

CASCADE Name of the settlement system used by Clearstream for German equity settlement.

Cash market A term used to describe the market where the cash asset trades, or the underlying market when talking about derivatives.

Cash sale A transaction on the floor of the stock exchange which calls for delivery of the securities that same day. In 'regular way' trades, the seller delivers securities on the fifth business day.

Cash settlement In the money market a transaction is said to be made for cash settlement if the securities purchased are delivered against payment on the same day the trade is made.

CAT CSD for Italian government bonds operated by the Bank of Italy.

CAVALI Depository and clearing organization for the Lima Stock Exchange.

CBLC Brazilian Clearing and Depository Corporation – clearing organization and CSD for BOVESPA.

CBOE Chicago Board Options Exchange.

CBOT Chicago Board of Trade.

CCASS Clearing system for the Stock Exchange of Hong Kong (Central Clearing and Settlement System).

CDP CSD for Singapore (Central Depository Pte).

CDS Canadian Depository for Securities.

CEDCOM Communication system operated by Clearstream.

Ceiling See **Cap**.

Central Depository System CSD for the Malaysian market.

Central Securities Depository An organization which holds securities in either immobilized or dematerialized form thereby enabling transactions to be processed by book entry transfer. Also provides securities administration services.

Certificate of deposit A money-market instrument.

CFTC The Commodities and Futures Commission (United States).

Chaps Clearing House Automated Payment System – clearing system for sterling and euro payments between banks.

Cheapest to deliver The cash security that provides the lowest cost (largest profit) to the arbitrage trader; the cheapest to deliver instrument is used to price the futures contract.

CHESS Organization for holding shares in dematerialized form in Australia (Clearing House Electronic Sub Register System).

Chinese walls Artificial barriers to the flow of information set up in large firms to prevent the movement of sensitive information between departments.

CHIPS Clearing House Interbank Payments System – clearing system for US dollar payments between banks in New York.

City code Principles and rules written by Panel on Takeovers and Mergers to regulate conduct during a takeover.

CLC Clearing organization and CSD for the Rio de Janeiro Stock Exchange.

Clean price The total price of a bond less accrued interest.

Clearance The process of determining accountability for the exchange of money and securities between counterparties to a trade: clearance creates statements of obligation for securities and/or funds due.

Clearance broker A broker who will handle the settlement of securities-related transactions for himself or another broker. Sometimes small brokerage firms may not clear for themselves and therefore employ the services of an outside clearing broker.

Clearing The centralized process whereby transacted business is recorded and positions are maintained.

Clearing house Company that acts as central counterparty for the settlement of stock exchange transactions. For example, on TD, Broker X sold 100, 300 and 500 securities of ABC and purchased 50 and 200 units of the same issue. The clearing system will net the transactions and debit X with 650 units (–900 + 250 = 650) against the total cash amount. This enables the broker to reduce the number of movements and thus the costs.

Clearing organization The clearing organization acts as the guarantor of the performance and settlement of contracts that are traded on an exchange.
Clearing system System established to clear transactions.
Clearstream CSD and clearing house based in Luxembourg and Frankfurt.
CLOB Dealing system of the Singapore Stock Exchange.
Close-ended Organizations such as companies which are a certain size as determined by their share capital.
Closing day In a new bond issue, the day when securities are delivered against payment by syndicate members participating in the offering.
Closing trade A bought or sold trade which is used to partly offset an open position, to reduce it or to fully offset it and close it.
CME Chicago Mercantile Exchange.
CMO Central Moneymarkets Office – clearing house and depository for UK money markets.
Collar Also cylinder, tunnel, fence or corridor. The sale of a put (or call) option and purchase of a call (or put) at different strikes (typically both out-of-the-money) or the purchase of a cap combined with the sale of a floor. See **Range forward**.
Collateral An acceptable asset used to cover a margin requirement.
Collateralized mortgage obligations Bonds backed by a pool of mortgages owned by the issuer. They usually reimburse capital at each coupon payment as per reimbursement of the underlying mortgages.
Commercial paper A money-market instrument.
Commission Charge levied by a firm for agency broking.
Commodity futures These comprise five main categories; agriculturals (e.g. wheat and potatoes), softs (e.g. coffee and cocoa), precious metals (e.g. gold and silver), non-ferrous metals (e.g. copper and lead), and energies (e.g. oil and gas).
Common stock Securities which represent ownership in a corporation. The two most important common stockholder rights are the voting right and dividend right. Common stockholders' claims on

corporate assets are subordinate to those of bondholders, preferred stockholders and general creditors.

Compliance officer Person appointed within an authorized firm to be responsible for ensuring compliance with the rules.

Compound interest Interest calculated on the assumption that interest amounts will be received periodically and can be reinvested (usually at the same rate).

Conduct of Business Rules Rules required by FSA 1986 to dictate how firms conduct their business. They deal mainly with the relationship between firm and client.

Confirm An agreement for each individual OTC transaction which has specific terms.

Conflicts of interest Circumstances that arise where a firm has an investment which could encourage it not to treat its clients favourably. The more areas in which a firm is involved, the greater the number of potential conflicts.

Continuous net settlement Extends multilateral netting to handle failed trades brought forward. See **Multilateral netting**.

Contract The standard unit of trading for futures and options. It is also commonly referred to as a 'lot'.

Contract for difference Contract designed to make a profit or avoid a loss by reference to movements in the price of an item. The underlying item cannot change hands.

Contract note Legal documentation sent by securities house to clients providing details of a transaction completed on their behalf.

Convergence The movement of the cash asset price toward the futures price as the expiration date of the futures contract approaches.

Conversion premium The effective extra cost of buying shares through exercising a convertible bond compared with buying the shares directly in the market. Usually expressed as percentage of the current market price of the shares.

Conversion price The normal value of a convertible which may be exchanged for one share.

Conversion ratio The number of shares into which a given amount (e.g. £100 or $1000) of the nominal value of a convertible can be converted.

Convertible bond Security (usually a bond or preferred stock) that can be exchanged for other securities, usually common stock of the same issuer, at the option of the holder and under certain conditions.

Convertible currency A currency that is freely convertible into another currency. Currencies for which domestic exchange control legislation specifically allows conversion into other currencies.

CORES Dealing system of the Singapore Stock Exchange.

Core rules Forty rules written by the FSA under the three-tier approach, to be universally applicable. Dedesignated in November 1994.

Corporate action One of many possible capital restructuring changes or similar actions taken by the company, which may have an impact on the market price of its securities, and which may require the shareholders to make certain decisions.

Corporate debt securities Bonds or commercial papers issued by private corporations.

Corporate finance General title which covers activities such as raising cash through new issues.

Correlation Refers to the degree to which fluctuations of one variable are similar to those of another.

Corridor See **Collar**.

Cost of carry The net running cost of holding a position (which may be negative) e.g., the cost of borrowing cash to buy a bond, less the coupon earned on the bond while holding it.

Counterparty A trade can take place between two or more counterparties. Usually one party to a trade refers to its trading partners as counterparties.

Coupon Generally, the nominal annual rate of interest expressed as a percentage of the principal value. The interest is paid to the holder of a fixed income security by the borrower. The coupon is generally paid annually, semi-annually or, in some cases, quarterly depending on the type of security.

Coupon swap An interest rate swap in which one leg is fixed-rate and the other is floating rate. See basis swap.

Covered option An option bought or sold offsetting an existing underlying position. See **Naked option**.

Credit creation Expansion of loans which in turn expands the money supply.

Credit derivatives Credit derivatives have as the underlying asset some kind of credit default. As with all derivatives, the credit derivative is designed to enable the risk related to a credit issue, such as non-payment of an interest coupon on a corporate or sovereign bond, or the non-repayment of a loan, to be transferred.

Credit risk The risk that a borrower, or a counterparty to a deal, or the issuer of a security, will default on repayment or not deliver its side of the deal.

CREST The organization in the UK that holds UK and Irish company shares in dematerialized form and clears and settles trades in UK and Irish company shares.

CRESTCo Organization that owns CREST.

CREST member A participant within CREST who holds stock in stock accounts in CREST and whose name appears on the share register. A member is their own *user*.

CREST-sponsored member A participant within CREST who holds stock in stock accounts in CREST and whose name appears on the share register. Unlike a member, a sponsored member is not their own user. The link to CREST is provided by another user who sponsors the sponsored member.

CREST user A participant within CREST who has an electronic link to CREST.

Cross-border trading Trading which takes place between persons or entities from different countries.

Cross-currency interest rate swap Same as currency swap.

Covered writing The sale of call options but the seller owns the stock which would be required to cover the delivery, if called.

Cross-currency interest rate swap An interest rate swap where the interest payments are in two different currencies and the exchange rate, for the final settlement, is agreed at the outset of the transaction.

Cum-dividend With dividend.

Cumulative preference share If the company fails to pay a preference dividend the entitlement to the dividend accumulates and the arrears of preference dividend must be paid before any ordinary dividend.

Currency exposure Currency exposure exists if assets are held or income earned in one currency while liabilities are denominated in another currency. The position is exposed to changes in the relative values of the two currencies such that the cost of the liabilities may be increased or the value of the assets or earning decreased.

Currency futures Contracts calling for delivery of a specific amount of a foreign currency at a specified future date in return for a given amount of, say, US dollars.

Currency swap An agreement to exchange interest related payments in the same currency from fixed rate into floating rate (or vice versa) or from one type of floating rate to another. A currency swap is different from an interest rate swap as the principal amounts are also swapped.

CUSIP The committee on Uniform Securities Identification Procedures, the body which established a consistent securities numbering system in the USA.

Custodian Institution holding securities in safekeeping for a client. A custodian also offers different services from its clients (settlement, portfolio services, etc.).

Customer – non-private Customer who is assumed to understand the workings of the investment world and therefore receives little protection from the Conduct of Business Rules.

Customer – private Customer who is assumed to be financially unsophisticated and therefore receives more protection from the Conduct of Business Rules.

Cylinder See **Collar**.

Daily cash sweep The action of investing a client's cash balance that would otherwise lie idle overnight, in an interest bearing deposit or investment vehicle. Generally performed on an overnight basis.

Daily Official List London Stock Exchange document which provides record of prices at which all stocks were traded on the previous day.

Day count fraction The proportion of a year by which an interest rate is multiplied in order to calculate the amount accrued or payable.

Dealer Individual or firm that acts as principal in all transactions, buying for his own account.

Debenture Another name for a corporate bond – usually secured on assets of the company.

Default Failure to perform on a futures contract, either cash settlement or physical settlement.

Deferred share A class of share where the holder is only entitled to a dividend if the ordinary shareholders have been paid a specified minimum dividend.

Definitive bond Any bond issued in final form. It is used particularly in reference to permanent bonds for which Temporary Bonds or Interim Certificates were issued.

Deliverable basket The list of securities which meets the delivery standards of futures contracts.

Delivery The physical movement of the underlying asset on which the derivative is based from seller to buyer.

Delivery versus payment Settlement where transfer of the security and payment for that security occur simultaneously.

Delta The sensitivity of an option price to changes in the price of the underlying product.

Demand deposit account A loan or checking account that gives its owner the right to withdraw funds from a commercial bank at his or her own discretion.

Dematerialized (form) Circumstances where securities are held in a book entry transfer system with no certificates.

Department of Trade and Industry Department of government responsible for some commercial matters including monopolies and prosecution of insider dealing.

Depository receipts Certificate issued by a bank in a country to represent shares of a foreign corporation issued in a foreign country. It entitles the holder to dividends and capital gains. They trade and pay dividends in the currency of the country of issuance of the certificate.

Depository Trust Company (DTC) A US central securities depository through which members may arrange deliveries of securities between each other through electronic debit and credit entries without the physical delivery of the securities. DTC is industry-owned with the NYSE as the majority owner. DTC is a member of the Federal Reserve System.

Derivative A financial instrument whose value is dependent upon the value of an underlying asset.

Deutsche Börse The German Stock Exchange.

Dilution Reducing the actual or potential earnings per share by issuing more shares or giving options to obtain them.

Direct market participant A broker, broker/dealer or any direct member of an exchange.

Direct placement Selling a new issue by placing it with one or several institutional investors rather than offering it for sale publicly.

Dirty price The total price of a bond including accrued interest.

Disclaimer A notice or statement intending to limit or avoid potential legal liability.

Discount The amount by which a future is priced below its theoretical price, or below the price of the underlying instrument.

Discount factor The number by which a future cash flow must be multiplied in order to calculate its present value.

Discount securities Non-interest-bearing short-term securities that are issued at discount and redeemed at maturity for full face value.

Diversification Investment strategy of spreading risk by investing the total available in a range of investments.

Dividend Distribution of profits made by a company if it chooses to do so.

Dividend per share Indicated annual dividend based on the most recently announced quarterly dividend times four plus any additional dividends to be paid during the current fiscal year.

Dividend yield The dividend expressed as a percentage of the share price.

DK Don't Know. Applies to a securities transaction pending settlement where fundamental data is missing which prevents the receiving party from accepting delivery.

Domestic bond Bond issued in the country of the issuer, in its country and according to the regulations of that country.

Double Taxation Treaty An agreement between two countries intended to avoid or limit the double taxation of income. Under the terms of the treaty an investor with tax liabilities in both countries can either apply for a reduction of taxes imposed by one country or can credit taxes paid in that country against tax liabilities in the other.

Dow Jones Index Main share index used in the USA.

Down-and-out option A knock-out option where the trigger is lower than the underlying rate at the start. See **Up-and-in option**.

Drop-lock A hybrid form of floating-rate note which converts into a fixed-rate bond once interest rates drop to a predetermined level.

DRP or (DRIP) Dividend Reinvestment Plan.

DTC Depository Trust Company – CSD for shares in the USA.

Duration A measure of the relative volatility of a bond; it is an approximation for the price change of a bond for a given change in the interest rate. Duration is measured in units of time. It includes the effects of time until maturity, cash flows and the yield to maturity.

ECB European Central Bank.

ECSDA European Central Securities Depository Association.

EFP Exchange of futures for physical. Common in the energy markets. A physical deal priced on the futures markets.

ELEX Dealing system of the Lima Stock Exchange.

EUCLID Communications system operated by Euroclear.

EUREX German–Swiss derivatives exchange created by the merger of the German (DTB) and Swiss (SOFFEX) exchanges.

EURONEXT An amalgamation of the Dutch, French and Belgium Exchanges.

Earnings per share (EPS) The total profit of a company divided by the number of shares in issue.

Effective date The date on which the interest period to which a FRA or swap relates, is to start.

Elective event Corporate action which requires a choice from the security owner.

Electronic order book The electronic order matching system used as the system for dealing in the shares which comprise the FT-SE 100 stock.

Embedded option An option which is included as part of a product.

Emerging market Non-industrialized country with:

- Low or middle per capita income, as published annually by the World Bank
- Undeveloped capital market (i.e. the market represents only a small portion of their GDP).

Endowment policy Form of saving linked with life assurance. Must be held for at least 10 years to get full benefit.

Equity A common term to describe stocks or shares.

Equity/stock options Contracts based on individual equities or shares. On exercise of the option the specified amount of shares are exchanged between the buyer and the seller through the clearing organization.

Equity index swap An obligation between two parties to exchange cash flows based on the percentage change in one or more stock indices, for a specific period with previously agreed reset dates. The swap is cash settled and based on notional principal amounts. One side of an equity swap can involve a LIBOR reference rate.

ERNIE Colloquial name for computer which selects the winners of premium bond prizes.

E-T-D This is the common term which is used to describe exchange traded derivatives which are the standardized products. It also differentiates products which are listed on an exchange as opposed to those offered over-the-counter.

ETF (exchange-traded funds) Passively managed basket of stocks that mirrors a particular index and that can be traded like ordinary shares. They trade intraday on stock exchanges, like securities, at market-determined prices. In essence, ETFs are index funds that trade like stocks.

EURIBOR A measure of the average cost of funds over the whole euro area based on a panel of 57 banks.

Euro The name of the single European currency.

Eurobond An interest-bearing security issued across national borders, usually issued in a currency other than that of the issuer's home country.

Euroclear A book-entry clearing facility for most eurocurrency and foreign securities. It is owned by a large number of banks of North American and European origin and is managed by Morgan Guaranty Trust in Brussels.

Euro-commercial Unsecured corporate debt with a short maturity structured to appeal to large financial institutions active in the euro market.

European monetary system (EMS) Agreement between most members of the common market on how to organize their currencies.

European style option An option which can only be exercised on the expiry day.

Exception-based processing Transaction processing where straightforward items are processed automatically, allowing staff to concentrate on the items which are incorrect or not straightforward.

Execution and clearing agreement An agreement signed between the client and the clearing broker. This sets out the terms by which the clearing broker will conduct business with the client.

Exchange Market place for trading.

Exchange delivery settlement price (EDSP) The price determined by the exchange for physical delivery of the underlying instrument or cash settlement.

Exchange owned clearing organization Exchange- or member-owned clearing organizations are structured so that the clearing members guarantee each other with the use of a member's default fund and additional funding like insurance, with no independent guarantee.

Exchange rate The rate at which one currency can be exchanged for another.

Exchange rate mechanism That part of the EMS that relates to pegging the rates against each other within predetermined limits.

Ex-date Date on or after which a sale of securities is executed without the right to receive dividends or other entitlements.

Ex-dividend Thirty-seven days before interest payment is due gilt-edged stocks are made 'ex-dividend'. After a stock has become 'ex-dividend', a buyer of stock purchases it without the right to receive the next (pending) interest payment.

Execute and eliminate order Type of order input into SETS. The amount that can be tracked immediately against displayed orders is completed, with the remainder being rejected.

Execution The action of trading in the markets.

Execution and clearing agreement An agreement signed between the client and the clearing broker. This sets out the terms by which the clearing broker will conduct business with the client.

Execution only or give-up agreement Tripartite agreement which is signed by the executing broker, the clearing broker and the client. This sets out the terms by which the clearing broker will accept business on behalf of the client.

Exercise The process by which the holder of an option may take up their right to buy or sell the underlying asset.

Exercise price (or strike price) The fixed price, per share or unit, at which an option conveys the right to call (purchase) or put (sell) the underlying shares or units.

Exotic options New generation of option derivatives, including look-backs, barriers, baskets, ladders, etc. They have different terms from standardized traded options.

Expiry date The last date on which an option holder can exercise their right. After this date an option is deemed to lapse or be abandoned.

Extraordinary general meeting (EGM) Any meeting of a company's shareholders other than its AGM.

Ex-warrants Trading a security so that the buyer will not be entitled to warrants that will be distributed to holders.

Face value The value of a bond, note, mortgage or other security that appears on the face of the issue, unless the value is otherwise specified by the issuing company. Face value is ordinarily the amount the issuing company promises to pay at maturity. It is also referred to as par value or nominal value.

Failed transaction A securities transaction that does not settle on time; i.e. the securities and/or cash are not exchanged as agreed on the settlement date.

Fair value For futures, it is the true price not the market price, allowing for the cost of carry. For options, it is the true price, not the market price, as calculated using an option pricing model.

Federal Reserve Book Entry System CSD for US government securities.

Fill or kill order Type of order input into SETS. It is either completed in full against displayed orders or rejected in full.

Final settlement The completion of a transaction when the delivery of all components of a trade is performed.

Financial futures/options contracts Financial futures is a term used to describe futures contracts based on financial instruments like currencies, debt instruments and financial indices.

Financial Services and Markets Act 2000 The legislation that created the single UK regulator, the Financial Services Authority.

Financial Services Authority (FSA) The agency designated by the Treasury to regulate investment business as required by the FSA 1986. It is the main regulator of the financial sector and was formerly called the Securities and Investments Board (SIB). It assumed its full powers on 1 December 2001.

First notice day The first day that the holders of short positions can give notification to the exchange/clearing house that they wish to effect delivery.

Fiscal agent A commercial bank appointed by the borrower to undertake certain duties related to the new issue, such as assisting the payment of interest and principal, redeeming bonds or coupons, handling taxes, replacement of lost or damaged securities, destruction of coupons and bonds once payments have been made

Fiscal years These run from 6 April to 5 April and are the periods of assessment for both income tax and capital gains tax.

Fit and proper Under the FSA 1986 everyone conducting investment business must be a 'fit and proper person'. The Act does not define the term, a function which is left to the regulators such as FSA.

Fixed income Interest on a security which is calculated as a constant specified percentage of the principal amount and paid at the end of specified interest periods, usually annually or semi-annually, until maturity.

Fixed leg In a coupon swap, the flow of a fixed-rate interest payment from one party to the other.

Fixed-rate A borrowing or investment where the interest or coupon paid is fixed throughout the arrangement. In a FRA or coupon swap, the fixed-rate is the fixed interest rate paid by one party to the other, in return for a floating-rate receipt (i.e. an interest rate that is to be refixed at some future time or times).

Fixed rate borrowing A fixed rate borrowing establishing the interest rate that will be paid throughout the life of the loan.

Fixed rate payer In a coupon swap, the party that pays the fixed rate.

Fixed rate receiver In a coupon swap, the party that receives the fixed rate.

Flat position A position which has been fully closed out and no liability to make or take delivery exists.

Flat yield The yield of a bond calculated as

$$\frac{\text{Annual coupon}}{\text{Current market price}} \times 100\%.$$

Also called the income yield.

Flex options Newly introduced contracts which are a cross between OTCs and exchange traded products. The advantage of flex options is that participants can choose various parts of the contract specification such as the expiry date and exercise price.

Floating leg In a coupon swap, the flow of a floating-rate interest payment from one party to the other.

Floating rate A borrowing or investment where the interest or coupon paid changes throughout the arrangement in line with some reference rate such as LIBOR. In a FRA or coupon swap, the floating rate is the floating interest rate (i.e. an interest rate that is to be refixed at some future time or times) paid by one party to the other, in return for a fixed-rate receipt.

Floating-rate note (FRN) Bond where each interest payment is made at the current or average market levels, often by reference to LIBOR.

Floating-rate payer Same as fixed-rate received in a coupon swap.

Floating-rate receiver Same as fixed rate payer in a coupon swap.

Floor A package of interest rate options whereby, at each of a series of future fixing dates, if an agreed reference rate such as LIBOR is lower than the strike rate, the option buyer received the difference between them, calculated on an agreed notional principal amount for the period until the next fixing date. See **Cap; collar**.

Floorbrokerage The process of delegating the execution of futures and options to another counterparty.

Foreign bond Bond issued in a domestic market in the domestic currency and under the domestic rules of issuance by a foreign issuer (ex. Samurai bonds are bonds issued by issuers of other countries on the Japanese market).

Forex Abbreviation for foreign exchange (currency trading).

Forward delivery Transactions which involve a delivery date in the future.

Forward rate agreements (FRAs) An agreement where the client can fix the rate of interest that will be applied to a notional loan or deposit, drawn or placed on an agreed date in the future, for a specified term.

Forwards These are very similar to futures contracts but they are not mainly traded on an exchange. They are not marked to market daily but settled only on the delivery date.

FSA Financial Services Authority.

FT-SE 100 index Main UK share index based on 100 leading shares.

FT-SE Mid 250 UK share index based on the 250 shares immediately below the top 100.

Fund manager An organization that invests money on behalf of someone else.

Fungibility A futures contract with identical administration in more than one financial centre. Trades in various geographical locations can be offset (e.g. bought on the IPE and sold on the SIMEX).

Future value The amount of money which can be achieved at a given date in the future by investing (or borrowing) a given sum of money now at a given interest rate, assuming compound reinvestment (or refunding) of any interest payments received (or paid) before the end.

Futures An agreement to buy or sell an asset at a certain time in the future for a certain price.

Futures and Options Fund (FOF) Type of authorized unit trust which can invest partially in derivatives.

Geared Futures and Options Fund (GFOF) Type of authorized unit trust which can invest in derivatives.

Gearing The characteristic of derivatives which enables a far greater reward for the same, or much smaller, initial outlay. It is the ratio of exposure to investment outlay, and is also known as leverage.

General principles Ten fundamental principles of behaviour written by the FSA to apply to all investment businesses.

Generic A generic swap is one for a standard period, against a standard fixing benchmark such as LIBOR.

Gilt Domestic sterling-denominated long-term bond backed by the full faith and credit of the UK and issued by the Treasury.

Gilt-edged market-makers (GEMMs) A firm that is a market-maker in gilts. Also known as a primary dealer.

Gilt-edged security UK government borrowing.

Give-up The process of giving a trade to a third party who will undertake the clearing and settlement of the trade.

Global bond A (temporary) certificate representing the whole of a bond issue.

Global clearing The channelling of the settlement of all futures and options trades through a single counterparty or through a number of counterparties geographically located.

Global custodian Institution that safekeeps, settles and performs processing of income collection, tax reclaim, multicurrency reporting, cash management, foreign exchange, corporate action and proxy monitoring etc. for clients' securities in all required marketplaces.

Global depository receipt (GDR) A security representing shares held in custody in the country of issue.

GLOBEX The overnight trading system operated by Reuters and the Chicago Mercantile Exchange (CME).

Good delivery Proper delivery of certificates that are negotiable and complete in terms of documentation or information.

Grey market Generally, the market for a new issue before the securities have been distributed to subscribers.

Gross A position which is held with both the bought and sold trades kept open.

Gross domestic product (GDP) A measure of the country's entire output.

Gross redemption yield (GRY) The annual return on owning a bond, allowing both for interest and profit on redemption.

Group Where one company controls one or more other companies, they are collectively a group.

Group of 30 (G30) Private international organization aiming to deepen understanding of international economic and financial issues.

GSCC Government Securities Clearing Corporation – clearing organization for US Treasury securities.

Guaranteed bond Bonds on which the principal or income or both are guaranteed by another corporation or parent company in case of default by the issuing corporation.

Haircut The discount applied to the value of collateral used to cover margins.

Hard commodities Commodities such as tin or zinc. Futures on them are traded on the London Metal Exchange.

Hedge ratio Determining the ratio of the futures to the cash position so as to reduce price risk.

Hedging A trading method which is designed to reduce or mitigate risk. Reducing the risk of a cash position in the futures instrument to offset the price movement of the cash asset. A broader definition of hedging includes using futures as a temporary substitute for the cash position.

Hit A dealer who agrees to sell at the bid price quoted by another dealer is said to hit that bid.

HKE The holding company of the Hong Kong Futures Exchange, The Stock Exchange of Hong Kong Ltd and The Hong Kong Securities Clearing Company Ltd.

Holder A person who buys a put or call option.

Holding company A company which owns more than 50% of the shares of another company as its holding company.

Home state regulation Under the ISD, an investment business is authorized in the place of its head office and registered office. This home state authorization entitles it to conduct business in any member state of the European Union.

Host state regulation Any European investment business operating outside its home basis is regulated by its host for its conduct of business.

ICOM International Currency Options Market: standard documentation for netting foreign exchange option settlements.

Immobilization The storage of securities certificates in a vault in order to eliminate physical movement of certificates/documents in transfer of ownership.

Implied repo rate The rate of return before financing costs implied by a transaction where a longer-term cash security is purchased and a futures contract is sold (or vice versa).

In-the-money A call option where the exercise price is below the underlying share price or a put option where the exercise price is above the underlying share price.

Independent clearing organization The independent organization is quite separate from the actual members of the exchange, and will guarantee to each member the performance of the contracts by having them registered in the organization's name.

Inflation A period of generally rising prices.

Index funds Unit trusts which invest in the constituent parts of an index.

Index linked bond Bond whose interest payment and redemption value are linked to the retail prices index.

Index swap Sometimes the same as a basis swap. Otherwise, a swap where payments on one or both of the legs are based on the value of an index, such as an equity index.

Indirect market participation Non-broker/dealers, such as institutional investors, who are active investors/traders.

Initial margin The deposit which the clearing house calls as protection against a default of a contract. It is returnable to the clearing member once the position is closed. The level is subject to changes in line with market conditions.

Insider dealing The criminal offence whereby those with unpublished price-sensitive information deal, advise others to deal or pass on the information. Maximum penalty is seven years in jail and an unlimited fine.

Institutional investor An institution which is usually investing money on behalf of others. Examples are mutual funds and pension funds.

Integration The third stage of money laundering, in which the money is finally integrated into the legitimate economy. See **Placement; Layering**.

Inter-bank market A market for transactions exclusively or predominantly within the banking system. In most countries, the market for short-term money is an Interbank market since banks borrow and lend among one another in order to balance their books on a daily basis. Non-bank entities may or may not be permitted to participate.

Inter dealer broker (IDB) Member of the London Stock Exchange that acts as a link between firms to enable them to trade with each other anonymously.

Interest rate cap An option product where the holder (buyer) is guaranteed a maximum borrowing cost over a specified term at a rate of his choosing. A premium is required.

Interest rate collar An option product where the holder (buyer) is guaranteed a maximum and minimum borrowing cost over a specified term at rates of his choosing. A premium may be required, but may net to zero. Involves the simultaneous trading of caps and floors.

Interest rate floor An option product where the holder (buyer) is guaranteed a minimum yield on a deposit over a specified term at a rate of his choosing. A premium is required.

Interest rate futures Based on a debt instrument such as a Government Bond or a Treasury Bill as the underlying product and require the delivery of a bond or bill to fulfil the contract.

Interest rate guarantee Also IRG. Effectively an option on a forward rate agreement. An IRG can be either a borrower's option (i.e. a call on an FRA) or a lender's option (i.e. a put on an FRA).

Interest rate swap An agreement to exchange interest-related payments in the same currency from fixed rate into floating rate (or vice versa) or from one type of floating rate to another.

Interim dividend Dividend paid part-way through a year in advance of the final dividend.

International depository receipt (IDR) Receipt of shares of a foreign corporation held in the vaults of a depository bank. The receipt entitles the holder to all dividends and capital gains. Dividends and capital gains are converted to local currency as part of the service. IDRs allow investors to purchase foreign shares without having to involve themselves in foreign settlements and currency conversion.

International equity An equity of a company based outside the UK but traded internationally.

International Petroleum Exchange (IPE) Market for derivatives of petrol and oil products.

International Securities Identification (ISIN) A coding system developed by the ISO for identifying securities. ISINs are designated to create one unique worldwide number for any security. It is a 12-digit alpha/numeric code.

International Standards Organization (ISO) An international federation of organizations of various industries which seeks to set common international standards in a variety of fields.

Interpolation The estimation of a price or rate, usually for a broken date, from two other rates or prices, each of which is for a date either side of the required date.

Intervention The process whereby the Bank of England acts to influence the exchange rate for sterling by buying it to support its value or selling it to weaken it.

In-the-money An option whose strike is more advantageous to the option buyer than the current market rate. See **At-the-money; out-of-the-money**.

Intra-day margin An extra margin call which the clearing organization can call during the day when there is a very large movement up or down in the price of the contract.

Intrinsic value The amount by which an option is in-the-money.

Investment business Dealing, advising or managing investments. Those doing so need to be authorized.

Investment Services Directive (ISD) European Union Directive imposing common standards on investment business.

Investment trust (company) A company whose sole function is to invest in the shares of other companies.

Investments Items defined in the FSA 86 to be regulated by it. Includes shares, bonds, options, futures, life assurance and pensions.

Investor Protection Committee (IPC) Divisions of the ABI and NAPF set up to monitor their positions as shareholders.

Invoice amount The amount calculated under the formula specified by the futures exchange which will be paid in settlement of the delivery of the underlying asset.

IOSCO International Organization of Securities Commissions.

IPMA International Primary Markets Association.

IRG See **Interest rate guarantee**.

Irredeemable gilt A gilt with no fixed date for redemption. Investors receive interest indefinitely.

IRS See **Interest rate swap**.

ISDA International Swaps and Derivatives Association, previously known as the International Swap Dealers Association. Many market participants use ISDA documentation.

ISMA International Securities Markets Association.

ISSA International Society of Securities Administrators.

ISSA The International Securities Services Association.

Issue Stocks or bonds sold by a corporation or government entity at a particular time.

Issue price The percentage of principal value at which the price of a new issue of securities is fixed.

Issuer Legal entity that issues and distributes securities.

Issuing agent Agent (e.g. bank) who puts out original issues for sale.

JASDEC Japan Securities Depository Centre – the CSD for Japan.

JATS Jakarta Automated Trading System.

JET Johannesburg Electronic Trading.

JSCC Japan Securities Clearing Corporation – clearing organization in Japan.

JSE Johannesburg Stock Exchange.

Junk bonds High-risk bonds that have low ratings or are in default.

Kas-Associate Settlement bank for the Netherlands.

KATS Dealing system for the Korean Stock Exchange.

KELER Clearing and depository for the Budapest Stock Exchange.

Knock-in-option An option which is activated if a trigger level is reached. See **Barrier option; knock-out option**.

Knock-out option An option which is cancelled if a trigger level is reached. See **Barrier option; knock-in option**.

Korea Securities Depository CSD and clearing organization for the Korean Stock Exchange.

Last notice day The final day that notification of delivery of a futures contract will be possible. On most exchanges all outstanding short futures contracts will be automatically delivered to open long positions.

Last trading day Often the day preceding last notice day which is the final opportunity for holders of long positions to trade out of their positions and avoid ultimate delivery.

Layering The second stage of money laundering, in which the money is passed through a series of transactions to obscure its origin. See **Placement; integration**.

LCH London Clearing House.

Lead managers In the eurobond markets the description given to the securities house appointed to handle a new issue.

Leverage The magnification of gains and losses by only paying for part of the underlying value of the instrument or asset; the smaller the amount of funds invested, the greater the leverage. It is also known as gearing.

LIBID The London inter-bank bid rate. The rate at which one bank will lend to another.

LIBOR The London inter-bank offered rate. It is the rate used when one bank borrows from another bank. It is the benchmark used to price many capital market and derivative transactions.

LIFFE London International Financial Futures and Options Exchange.

LIFFE Connect LIFFE electronic dealing system.

Limit order Type of order input into SETS. If not completed immediately the balance is displayed on the screen and forms the Order Book.

Line of credit A commitment by a bank to make loans to borrowers up to a specified maximum during a specified period.

Line order An order in which a customer sets the maximum price he or she is willing to pay as a buyer or the minimum price he is willing to accept as a seller.

Linked Forex When the currency contract is purchased to cover the local cost of a security trade.

Liquidity A liquid asset is one that can be converted easily and rapidly into cash without a substantial loss of value. In the money market, a security is said to be liquid if the spread between bid and asked price is narrow and reasonable size can be done at those quotes.

Liquidity risk The risk that a bank may not be able to close out a position because the market is illiquid.

Listed company Company which has been admitted to listing on a stock exchange and whose shares can then be dealt on that exchange.

Listed securities Securities listed on a stock exchange are tradeable on this exchange.

Listing Status applied for by companies whose securities are then listed on the London Stock Exchange and available to be traded.

Listing particulars Detailed information that must be published by a company applying to be listed.

Listing rules Rule book for listed companies which governs their behaviour. Commonly known as the Yellow Book.

Liquidity Ease with which an item can be traded on the market. Liquid markets are described as deep.

Lloyd's of London The world's largest insurance market.

Loan stock See **Bonds**.

Local An individual member of an exchange who trades solely for their own account.

London Inter-Bank Offer Rate (LIBOR) Rate at which banks lend to each other which is often used as the benchmark for floating-rate loans (FRNs).

London International Financial Futures and Options Exchange (LIFFE) Market for trading in bond, interest rate, FT-SE 100 index and FT-SE Mid 250 index, futures, plus equity options and soft commodity derivatives.

London Metal Exchange (LME) Market for trading in derivatives of metals such as copper, tin, zinc, etc.

London Stock Exchange (LSE) Market for trading in securities. Formerly know as the International Stock Exchange of the United Kingdom and Republic of Ireland or ISE.

Long A bought position in a derivative which is held open.

Long coupons (1) Bonds or notes with a long current maturity; (2) a coupon on which the period is longer than the others or the standard coupon period.

Long-dated Gilts with more than 15 years until redemption.

Long position Refers to an investor's account in which he or she has more shares of a specific security than he needs to meet his settlement obligations.

Lot The common term used to describe the standard unit of trading for futures and options. It is also referred to as a 'contract'.

Mandatory event A corporate action which affects the securities without giving any choice to the security holder.

Mandatory quote period Time of day during which market-makers in equities are obliged to quote prices under London Stock Exchange rules.

MAOS Dealing system of the Prague Stock Exchange.

Margin Money that must be deposited by participants in options and futures markets as a guarantee that they will be able to meet their commitments at the due date.

Mark-to-market The process of revaluing an OTC or exchange traded product each day. It is the difference between the closing price on the previous day against the current closing price. For exchange traded products this is referred to as variation margin.

Market Description of any organization or facility through which items are traded. All exchanges are markets.

Market counterparty A person dealing as agent or principal with the broker and involved in the same nature of investment business as the broker. This also includes fellow members of the SFA or trading members of an investment exchange, for those products only where they are members.

Market forces Supply and demand allowing buyers and sellers to fix the price without external interference.

Market-maker A trader who works for an organization such as an investment bank. They quote bids and offers in the market and are normally under an obligation to make a price in a certain number of contracts. They create liquidity in the contract by offering to buy or sell.

Market price In the case of a security, the market price is usually considered as the last reported price at which the stock or bond has been sold.

Market risk Also position risk. The risk that the market value of a position falls.

Market value The price at which a security is trading and could presumably be purchased or sold.

Master agreement This agreement is for OTC transactions and is signed between the client and the broker. It covers the basic terms under which the client and broker wish to transact business. Each individual trade has a separate individual agreement with specific terms known as a confirm.

Matching (comparison) Another term for comparison (or checking); a matching system to compare trades and ensure that both sides of trade correspond.

MATIF French derivatives exchange now part of EURONEXT.

Maturity The date on which the principal or nominal value of a bond becomes due and payable in full to the holder.

MCSD Clearing house and depository for the Egyptian Stock Exchange.

Medium dated Gilts due to be redeemed within the next 7 to 15 years.

Mercato Azionario di Borsa The listed market of the Milan Stock Exchange.

Mergers and Acquisition (M&A) Divisions of securities houses or merchant banks responsible for advising on take-over activity. Usually work with the corporate finance department and is often kept as a single unit.

Merval Trading and settlement organization for the Buenos Aires Stock Exchange. The trading system is called SINAC.

Mixed economy Economy which relies on a mix of market forces and government involvement.

MMTS Dealing system for the Budapest Stock Exchange.

Model risk The risk that the computer model used by a bank for valuation or risk assessment is incorrect or misinterpreted.

Model Code for Securities Dealing Part of the Yellow Book that relates to directors dealing in their own company's securities. Prohibits them from doing so during the two months before results are announced.

Modified following The convention that if a settlement date in the future falls on a non-business day, the settlement date will be moved to the next following business day, unless this moves it to the next month, in which case the settlement date is moved back to the last previous business day.

Money market The market for the purchase and sale of short-term financial instruments. Short term is usually defined as less than one year.

Money market fund An open-ended mutual fund which invests in commercial paper, bankers' acceptances, repurchase agreements, government securities, and other highly liquid and safe securities. The fund pays money market rates of interest. Many money market funds are part of fund families; investors can switch their money from one fund to another and back again without charge.

Money rate of return Annual return as a percentage of asset value.

Money supply Measure of the money available in the economy.

M0 & M4 Measure of the money supply which measures notes and coins (M0 or M0 Plus) and bank and building society deposits (M4).

MOF The Ministry of Finance (Japan).

Monti Titoli CSD for Italian securities.

Moody's Investment Service Located in New York City with its parent, Dun & Bradstreet, Moody's is one of the two most popular bond rating agencies in the USA. The other agency is Standard & Poor's.

Mortgage A form of security on borrowing commonly associated with home borrowing.

Mortgage-backed security Security backed by an investment company that raises money from shareholders and invests it in stocks, bonds or other instruments (unit trust, investment fund, SICAV–BEVEK).

MTA Dealing system of the Milan Stock Exchange.

Multilateral netting Trade between several counterparties in the same security are netted such that each counterparty makes only one transfer of cash or securities to another party or to a central clearing system. Handles only transactions due for settlement on the same day.

Mutual collateralization The deposit of collateral by both counterparties to a transaction.

Naked option An option bought or sold for speculation, with no offsetting existing position behind it.

Naked writing Where the seller does not own the stock corresponding to the call option which he or she has sold and would be forced to pay the prevailing market price for the stock to meet delivery obligations, if called.

Names Individuals of Lloyd's of London who join together in syndicates to write insurance business. Their liability is unlimited and therefore all their personal wealth is at risk.

NASDAQ National Association of Securities Dealers Automated Quotation system.

National Association of Pension Funds (NAPF) Trade association of pension funds through which they can voice their opinions collectively.

National Savings Department of government responsible for running a variety of short-term borrowings. Its operations are undertaken through the Post Office.

National Securities Depository Depository for the National Stock Exchange in India.

NECIGEF CSD for the Netherlands.

Net asset value (NAV) In mutual funds, the market value of the fund share. It is common practice for an investment trust to compute its assets daily, or even twice a day, by totalling the closing market value of all securities and assets (i.e. cash) owned. All liabilities are deducted, and the balance is divided by the number of shares outstanding. The resulting figure is the net asset value per share.

Net present value (NPV) The net total of several present values (arising from cashflows at different future dates) added together, some of which may be positive and some negative.

Netting Trading partners offset their positions thereby reducing the number of positions for settlement. Netting can be either *bilateral*, *multilateral* or *continuous net settlement*.

New issues Company raised additional capital by issuing new securities. New issue is the name given to the bonds or stocks offered to investors for the first time.

NIEC Another CSD in the Netherlands.

Nikkei Dow Index Main share index in Japan.

Nil paid rights price Ex-rights price less the subscription price.

Nominal amount Value stated on the face of a security (principal value, par value). Securities processing: number of securities to deliver/receive.

Nominal value of a bond The value at which the capital, or principal, of a bond will be redeemed by the issuer. Also called par value.

Nominal value of a share The minimum price at which a share can be issued. Also called par value.

Nominated advisor Firm appointed to advise AIM company directors on their responsibilities. Role can be combined with that of nominated broker.

Nominated broker Firm appointed to assist dealing in AIM securities.

Nominee An organization that acts as the named owner of securities on behalf of a different beneficial owner who remains anonymous to the company.

Non-callable Cannot be redeemed by the issuer for a stated period of time from date of issue.

Non-clearing member A member of an exchange who does not undertake to settle their derivatives business. This type of member must appoint a clearing member to register all their trades at the clearing organization.

Non-competitive bid In an auction, bidding for a specific amount of securities without mentioning a price. Usually, the price paid will be equal to the average of the accepted competitive bids.

Non-cumulative preference share If the company fails to pay a preference dividend the entitlement to the dividend is simply lost. There is no accumulation.

Non-deliverable forward A foreign exchange forward outright where, instead of each party delivering the full amount of currency at settlement, there is a single net cash payment to reflect the change in value between the forward rates transacted and the spot rate two working days before settlement.

Non-private customer A person who is not a private customer or who has requested to be treated as a non-private customer.

Normal market size (NMS) Minimum size in which market-makers must quote on LSE.

Nostro A bank's nostro account is its currency account held at another bank.

Nostro reconciliation Checking the entries shown on the bank's nostro account statement with the bank's internal records (the accounting ledgers) to ensure that they correspond exactly.

Note Bonds issued with a relatively short maturity are often called notes.

Notional Contracts for differences require a notional principal amount on which settlement can be calculated.

Novation The process where registered trades are cancelled with the clearing members and substituted by two new ones – one between the clearing house and the clearing member seller, the other between the clearing house and the clearing member buyer.

NSCC National Securities Clearing Corporation – clearing organization for US shares.

OASYS Trade confirmation system for US brokers operated by Thomson Financial Services.

OATs Obligations Assimilables du Trésor – a 7–10-year French Treasury bond.

Obligation netting An arrangement to transfer only the net amount (of cash or a security) due between two or more parties, rather than transfer all amounts between the parties on a gross basis.

Off-balance sheet A transaction whose principal amount is not shown on the balance sheet because it is a contingent liability or settled as a contract for differences.

Offer for sale Historically, the most popular form of new issue in the UK for companies bringing their securities to the stock market for the first time. The company offers its shares to the general public.

Offer price The price at which a trader or market-maker is willing to sell a contract.

Office of Fair Trading (OFT) Government department which advises the Secretary of State for Trade and Industry on whether or not a proposed take-over should be referred to the MMC for full investigation.

Offshore Relates to locations outside the controls of domestic monetary, exchange and legislative authorities. Offshore may not necessarily be outside the national boundaries of a country. In some countries, certain banks or other institutions may be granted offshore status and thus be exempt from all or specific controls or legislation.

Omnibus account Account containing the holdings of more than one client.

On-balance sheet A transaction whose principal amount is shown on the balance sheet.

On-line Processing which is executed via an interactive input onto a PC or stationary terminal connected to a processing centre.

Open economy A country where there are no restrictions on trading with other countries.

Open-ended Type of investment such as Unit Trusts or OEICs which can expand without limit.

Open-ended investment company (OEIC) New corporate structure introduced in 1997. It is a form of collective investment vehicle.

Open interest The number of contracts both bought and sold which remain open for delivery on an exchange. Important indicator for liquidity.

Open outcry The style of trading whereby traders face each other in a designated area such as a pit and shout or call their respective bids and offers. Hand signals are also used to communicate. It is governed by exchange rules.

Open position The number of contracts which have not been offset at the clearing organization by the close of business.

Opening trade A bought or sold trade which is held open to create a position.

Operational risk The risk of losses resulting from inadequate systems and control, human errors or management failings.

Option An option is, in the case of the *buyer*, the right, but not the obligation, to take (call) or make (put) for delivery of the underlying product and, in the case of the *seller*, the obligation to make or take delivery of the underlying product.

Option premium The sum of money paid by the buyer for acquiring the right of the option. It is the sum of money received by the seller for incurring the obligation, having sold the rights, of the option. It is the sum of the intrinsic value and the time value.

Optional dividend Dividend that can be paid either in cash or in stock. The shareholders entitled to the dividend make the choice.

Options on futures These have the same characteristics as an option, the difference being that the underlying product is either a long or short futures contract. Premium is not exchanged as the contracts are marked to market each day.

Order-driven market A stock market where brokers acting on behalf of clients match trades with each other either on the trading floor of the exchange or through a central computer system.

Out of pocket expenses Market charges which are charged to the client without taking any profit.

Out-of-the-money A call option whose exercise price is above the current underlying share price or a put option whose exercise price is below the current underlying share price. This option has no intrinsic value.

Out-trade A trade which has been incorrectly matched on the floor of an exchange.

Over-the-counter (OTC) A one-to-one agreement between two counterparties where the specifications of the product are completely flexible and non-standardized.

Over-the-counter trading Trading made outside a stock exchange.

Overdraft Withdrawal of more money than is in a bank account at a given time.

Overnight money Money placed on the money market for repayment for the next day.

Oversubscribed Circumstances where people have applied for more shares than are available in a new issue.

Panel on Takeovers and Mergers (PTM) A non-statutory body comprising City institution which regulates take-over activities.

Par value See **Nominal value of a bond/share**.

Pair off Back-to-back trade between two parties where settlement occurs only by exchanging the cash difference between the two parties.

Pari passu Without partiality. Securities that rank *pari passu* rank equally with each other.

Paying agent A bank which handles payment of interest and dividends on behalf of the issuer of a security.

Payment date Date on which a dividend or an interest payment is scheduled to be paid.

Pension fund Fund set up by a corporation, trade union, governmental entity or other organization to pay the pension benefits of retired workers. Pension funds invest billions of dollars annually in the securities markets and are therefore major market players.

Perpetual bond A bond which has no redemption date.

Personal Equity Plan (PEP) Investment scheme whereby investors buy shares through a PEP manager; all profits and dividends are tax free.

Pit The designated area on the market floor where a particular contract is traded. It may be termed a ring in some markets, e.g. LME.

Placement The first stage of money laundering, in which the money is placed in the banking system. See **Layering; Integration**.

Placing Procedure used for new issues where a securities house contracts its own clients to offer them stock. It is almost always used for new issues of eurobonds and for equities on the London Stock Exchange more so since January 1996 when restrictions on their use were removed.

Plain vanilla or vanilla swap A swap which has a very basic structure.

Poison pill Strategic move by a company that is the target of a take-over to make its stock less attractive to an acquirer. As a defence, the company can issue poison pill rights.

Portfolio List of investments held by an individual or company, or list of loans made by a bank or financial institution.

Power of attorney The legal authority for one party to sign for and act on behalf of another party.

Preference shares Shares that have preferential rights to dividends, usually a fixed sum, before dividends are paid out to ordinary shareholders. They usually carry no voting rights. The rights of preference shareholders are established in a company's articles of association and may differ between companies in a variety of ways.

Premium An option premium is the amount paid upfront by the purchaser of the option to the writer.

Present value The amount of money which needs to be invested (or borrowed) now at a given interest rate in order to achieve exactly a given cashflow in the future, assuming compound reinvestment (or refunding) of any interest payments received (or paid) before the end. See **Future value**.

Pre-settlement Checks and procedures undertaken immediately after execution of a trade prior to settlement.

Price/earnings ratio The share price of a company divided by its earnings per share. A high p/e ratio implies that the company is well thought of for its future prospects.

Price (conversion) factor The price at which a bond would trade, per 1 nominal, to yield the notional coupon of the futures contract on the delivery day (or the first day in the deliverable month if this applies).

Primary dealer See **Gilt-edged market-maker**.

Primary market Market for the placement of new securities such as international, domestic and foreign bond issues. Any subsequent resale or purchase is handled on the secondary market.

Principal protected product An investment whose maturity value is guaranteed to be at least the principal amount invested initially.

Principal trading When a member firm of the London Stock Exchange buys stock from or sells stock to a non-member.

Principal-to-principal market A market where the clearing house only recognizes the clearing member as one entity, and not the underlying clients of the clearing member.

Principal value That amount inscribed on the face of a security and exclusive of interest or premium. The amount is the one used in the computation of interest due on such a security.

Private customer An individual person who is not acting in the course of carrying on investment business.

Private placement Issue of securities that is offered to a limited number of investors.

Privatization Process whereby the government puts state owned industries into the private sector, e.g. water, electricity. Usually involves an offer for sale of its shares.

Project A The after-hours trading system used by the CBOT.

Proprietary trader A trader who deals for an organization such as an investment bank taking advantage of short-term price movements as well as taking long-term views on whether the market will move up or down.

Prospectus See **Listing Particulars**.

Proxy Appointee of a shareholder who votes on his behalf at company meetings.

Public offering Offer of securities to the general public.

Public placement An issue of securities that is offered through a securities house to institutional and individual clients.

Public sector net cash requirement (PSNCR) Shortfall of government revenue over expenditure, which it needs to borrow. (This shortfall was until June 1998 known as the Public Sector Borrowing Requirement – PSBR.)

Put option An option that gives the buyer the right, but not the obligation, to sell a specified quantity of the underlying asset at a fixed price, on or before a specified date. The seller of a put option has the obligation (because they have sold the right) to take delivery of the underlying asset if the option is exercised by the buyer.

Quoted Colloquial term for a security that is traded on the Stock Exchange.

Quote driven Dealing system where some firms accept the responsibility to quote buying and selling prices.

Range forward A forward outright with two forward rates, where settlement takes place at the higher forward rate if the spot rate at maturity is higher than that, at the lower forward rate if the spot rate at maturity is lower than that, or at the spot rate at maturity otherwise. See **Collar**.

Rating Evaluation of securities investment and credit risk by rating services such as Moody's or Standard & Poor's.

RCH Recognized Clearing House under the Financial Services Act.

Real time gross settlement Gross settlement system where trades are settled continuously through the processing day – abbreviated to RTGS.

Realized profit Profit which has arisen from a real sale.

Recognized Investment Exchange (RIE) Status required by the FSA 1986 for exchanges in the UK.

Reconciliation The comparison of a person's records of cash and securities position with records held by another party and the investigation and resolution of any discrepancies between the two sets of records.

Record date The date on which a securities holder must hold the securities in order to receive an income or entitlement.

Redemption The purchase and cancellation of outstanding securities through a cash payment to the holder.

Redemption price A price at which bonds may be redeemed, or called, at the issuer's option, prior to maturity (often with a slight premium).

Referral If a proposed take-over is investigated thoroughly by the MMC the procedure is that it is referred to the MMC by the Secretary of State for Trade and Industry .

Registered bond A bond whose owner is registered with the issuer or its registrar.

Registered title Form of ownership of securities where the owner's name appears on a register maintained by the company.

Registrar An official of a company who maintains its share register.

Registrar of Companies Government department responsible for keeping records of all companies.

RELIT Settlement system used in France for corporate securities and OATS.

Reorganization Generally any event where the equity, debt or capital structure of a company is changed.

Replacement cost The mark-to-market loss which would be incurred if it were necessary to undertake a new transaction to replace an existing one, because the existing counterparty defaulted.

Repurchase agreement (Repo) Borrowing funds by providing a government security for collateral and promising to 'repurchase' the security at the end of the agreed upon time period. The associated interest rate is the 'repo-rate'.

Reputational risk The risk that an organization's reputation will be damaged.
Resolution Proposal on which shareholders vote put to them at a meeting.
Retail Price Index (RPI) Index that shows the movement of prices in the UK.
Reverse repo Purchase of gilt where the price and date for its resale is fixed at the same time.
RIE Recognized Investment Exchange under the Financial Services Act.
Right of offset Where positions and cash held by the clearing organization in different accounts for a member are allowed to be netted.
Rights issue Offer of shares made to existing shareholders.
Risk warning Document that must be despatched and signed by private customers before they deal in traded options.
Risk-weighted assets See **Capital adequacy**.
Rollercoaster swap A swap in which the notional principal amount varies up and down over the life of the swap.
Rolling settlement System used in most countries including England. Bargains are settled a set number of days after being transacted.
Roll-over A LIBOR fixing on a new tranche of loan, or transfer of a futures position to the next delivery month.
Round lot The minimum amount for which dealer's quotes are good.
Running a book Firms who are buying and selling stock for themselves hoping to profit from price differences are said to run a book in that stock.
Safekeeping Holding of securities on behalf of clients. They are free to sell at any time.
Sale of rights nil paid The sale of the entitlement to take up a rights issue. See also **Nil paid price**.
Same day funds Refers to the availability of funds on the same day as they are deposited.
Samurai bond A bond denominated in Japanese yen and issued in the Japanese capital market by a foreign borrower.

SATURNE Settlement system for BTANs and BTFs operated by the Banque de France.

Sawtooth risk A swap in which the notional principal amount varies up and down over the life of the swap, with an overall upward or downward trend.

SAX Dealing system of the Swedish Stock Exchange.

Scaling down When a new issue is oversubscribed, the procedure whereby applicants receive a proportion of the number of shares for which they applied.

SCANS Clearing and settlement system for Malaysia.

SCL Settlement organization and custodian of Spanish securities.

SCORE Dealing system for the Kuala Lumpur Stock Exchange.

Scrip dividends Scrip dividends options provide shareholders with the choice of receiving dividend entitlements in the form of cash, share or a combination or both. The amount of stocks to be distributed under a scrip option is calculated by dividing the cash dividend amount by the average market price over a recent period of time.

Scrip issue See **Bonus issue**.

SD Indeval Clearing house and depository for the Mexican market.

SEATS Plus An order-driven system used on the London Stock Exchange for securities which do not attract at least two firms of market-makers and for all AIM securities.

Secondary market Marketplace for trading in existing securities. The price at which they are trading has no direct effect on the company's fortunes but is a reflection of investors' perceptions of the company.

Securities Bonds and equities.

Securities and Futures Authority (SFA) The SRO responsible for regulating securities and futures firms prior to the FSA assuming its full powers.

Securities and Investments Board (SIB) Former name of the Financial Services Authority.

Securities house General term covering any type of organization involved in securities, although usually reserved for the larger firms.

Securities lending Loan of securities by an investor to another (usually a broker-dealer), usually to cover a short sale.

SEDOL Stock Exchange Daily Official List, a securities numbering system assigned by the International Stock Exchange in London.

Segregated account Account in which there are only the holdings of one client.

Segregation of funds Where the client assets are held separately from those assets belonging to the member firm.

SEHK Stock Exchange of Hong Kong.

Selective Marketing See **Placing**.

Self-regulating organizations (SROs) Bodies which receive their status from the FSA and are able to regulate sectors of the financial services industry. Membership of an SRO provides authorization.

SENN Dealing system for the Rio de Janeiro Stock Exchange.

SEQUAL The checking system used for international equities.

SET Stock Exchange of Thailand.

SETS London Stock Exchange Trading System.

Settlement The fulfilment of the contractual commitments of transacted business.

Settlement date The date on which a trade is cleared by delivery of securities against funds (actual settlement date, contractual settlement date).

17F-5 Legal requirements for world-wide correspondent banks which serve US mutual funds, pension funds and other regulated financial groups.

SGX The merged central Stock Exchange of Singapore & SIMEX.

Share futures Based on individual shares. Delivery is fulfilled by the payment or receipt of cash against the exchange calculated delivery settlement price.

Share option A right sold to an investor conferring the option to buy or sell shares of a particular company at a predetermined price and within a specified time limit.

Shogun bond Straight bond denominated in foreign currency, other than Japanese Yen, issued by a foreign issuer on the Japanese capital market.

Short A sold position in a derivative which is held open.

Short coupons Bonds or notes with a short current maturity.

Short cover The purchase of a security that has been previously sold short. The purpose is to return securities that were borrowed to make a delivery.

Short-dated gilt Gilts due to be redeemed within the next 7 years, according to the LSE (FT states up to 5 years).

Short sale The sale of securities not owned by the seller in the expectation that the price of these securities will fall or as part of an arbitrage.

Short selling Selling stock that you do not own.

Short-term security Generally an obligation maturing in less than one year.

Short-termism Allegation made against fund managers that they expect prices of shares in which they have invested to rise quickly and are not willing to exert influence on management to improve corporate performance but prefer to sell the shares.

SIBE Electronic dealing system linking the four Spanish stock exchanges.

SICOVAM CSD for French corporate securities and OATs (now merged with Euroclear).

Simple interest Interest calculated on the assumption that there is no opportunity to reinvest the interest payments during the life of an investment and thereby earn extra income.

SINAC Trading system for the Buenos Aires Stock Exchange. Operated by Merval.

Single currency interest rate swap An interest rate swap where the interest payments are exchanged in the same currency.

Sinking fund In the case of a loan repaid by instalments, each instalment can be considered to consist of two parts. One portion of each instalment represents the interest payable on the loan, the other portion, which represents the repayment of capital, is known as the 'sinking fund'.

SIS SEGA Inter Settle – CSD for Switzerland.

Soft commodities Description given to commodities such as sugar, coffee and cocoa, traded through LIFFE since its incorporation of the former London Commodity Exchange (LCE).

Sovereign debt securities Bonds issued by the government of a country.

SPAN Standardized Portfolio Analysis of Risk. A form of margin calculation which is used by various clearing organizations.

Speculation A deal undertaken because the dealer expects prices to move in his favour and thereby realize a profit.

Speculator The speculator is a trader who wants to assume risk for potentially much higher rewards.

Sponsored member Type of CREST member whose name appears on the register but has no computer link with CREST.

Spot delivery A delivery or settlement of currencies on the value date, two business days later.

Spot market Market for immediate as opposed to future delivery. In the spot market for foreign exchange, settlement is in two business days ahead.

Spot month The first month for which futures contracts are available.

Spot rate The price prevailing in the spot market.

SSCCR Shanghai Securities Central Clearing and Registration Corporation.

SSRC Shenzhen Securities Registration Company – clearing organization for the Shenzhen Stock Exchange.

Stag Someone who applies for a new issues of shares intending to sell them (at a profit) as soon as secondary market dealings start.

Stamp duty Tax on purchase of equities in the UK.

Stamp Duty Reserve Tax (SDRT) (UK) Tax payable on the purchase of UK equities in uncertified form (i.e. those held within CREST).

Standard settlement instructions Instructions for settlement with a particular counterparty which are always followed for a particular kind of deal and, once in place, are therefore not repeated at the time of each transaction.

Standing instruction Default instruction, e.g. provided to an agent processing payments or clearing securities trades; provided by shareholder on how to vote shares (for example, vote for all management recommended candidates).

Stanza di Compensazione Italian clearing organization.

State-controlled economy Country where all aspects of activity are controlled by the government.

Stepped A stepped coupon is one which rises or falls in a predetermined way over the life of an arrangement.

Stock In some countries (e.g. the USA), the term applies to ordinary share capital of a company. In other countries (e.g. the UK), stock may mean share capital that is issued in variable amounts instead of in fixed specified amounts, or it can describe government loans.

Stock dividend Dividends paid by a company in stock instead of cash.

Stock Exchange Automated Quotation System (SEAQ) Electronic screen display system through which market-makers in equities display prices at which they are willing to deal.

Stock Exchange Clearing House Clearing house for the Tel Aviv Stock exchange.

Stock Exchange Electronic Trading System (SETS) Stock-market Description usually given to the London Stock Exchange.

Stock Index Futures/Options Based on the value of an underlying stock index like the FTSE 100 in the UK, the S&P 500 index in the USA and the Nikkei 225 and 300 in Japan. Delivery is fulfilled by the payment or receipt of cash against the exchange calculated delivery settlement price. These are referred to as both indices or indexes.

Stock (order) An owner of a physical security that has been mutilated, lost or stolen will request the issuer to place a stop (transfer) on the security and to cancel and replace the security.

Stock (or bond) power A legal document, either on the back of registered stocks and bonds or attached to them, by which the owner assigns his interest in the corporation to a third party, allowing that party the right to substitute another name on the company records instead of the original owner's.

Stock split When a corporation splits its stock, which increases the number of shares in issue and has the effect of reducing the share price initially. The value of the investors overall holding remains unchanged.

Straddle The purchase of a call combined with the purchase of a put at the same strike (generally purchased with both at-the-money).

Straight debt A standard bond issue, without right to convert into the common shares of the issuer.

Straight-through processing Computer transmission of the details of a trade, without manual intervention, from their original input by the trader to all other relevant areas – position keeping, risk control, accounts, settlement, reconciliation.

STRATE New electronic settlement and depository organization for the Johannesburg Stock Exchange (Share Transactions Totally Electronic).

Street name Securities held in street name are held in the name of a broker or another nominee, i.e. a customer.

Strike price The fixed price, per share or unit, at which an option conveys the right to call (purchase) or put (sell) the underlying shares or units.

Strike price/rate Also exercise price. The price or rate at which the holder of an option can insist on the underlying transaction being fulfilled.

Strip The purchase or sale of a series of consecutive interest rate futures contracts or forward rate agreements.

Stripped bonds (strips) Bonds where the rights to the interest payments and eventual repayment of the nominal value have been separated from each other and trade independently. Facility introduced for gilts in December 1997.

Stump period A calculation period, usually at the beginning or end of a swap, other than the standard ones normally quoted.

Sub-custodian A bank in a foreign country that acts on behalf of the custodian as its custody agent.

Subscription price Price at which shareholders of a corporation are entitled to purchase common shares in a rights offering or at which subscription warrants are exercisable.

Subscriptions In a bond issue, the buying orders from the lead manager, co managers, underwriters and selling group members for the securities being offered.

Subsidiary A company, at least 50% of which is owned by another company. See **Holding Company**.

SuperDot Electronic order routing system on the New York Stock Exchange.

Swap Arrangement where two borrowers, one of whom has fixed interest and one of whom has floating rate borrowings, swap their commitments with each other. A bank would arrange the swap and charge a fee.

SwapClear A clearing house and central counterparty for swaps.

SwapsWire An electronic dealing system for swaps.

Swaption An option into a predetermined swap transaction. Options can be payers or receivers, American or European.

SWIFT Society for Worldwide Interbank Financial Telecommunications – secure electronic communications network between banks.

SWX Swiss Stock Exchange.

SYCOM The trading system operated by the Sydney Futures Exchange (SFE).

Syndicate A group of bond houses which act together in underwriting and distributing a new securities issue.

TACT Dealing system for the Tel Aviv Stock Exchange (Tel Aviv Continuous Trading).

Take-over When one company obtains more than 50% of another company's shares.

TARGET Trans European Automated Real time Gross settlement Express Transfer – system linking the real-time gross settlements for euros in the 15 European Union countries.

Tax Exempt Special Savings Account (TESSA) Scheme whereby certain savings plans will generate interest, free of income tax (now unavailable).

Tax reclaim The process that a global custodian and/or a holder of securities performs, in accordance with local government filing requirements, in order to recapture an allowable percentage of taxed withheld.

TechMark Market on the LSE for technology-related stocks.

Tender Offer Formal offer to buy made to holders of a particular issue by a third party. Detailed offer is made by public announcement in newspapers and sometimes by personal letter of transmittal to each stockholder.

Term insurance Insurance that pays the insurer's beneficiary on death. There is no savings element.

Termination date The end date of a swap.

Terms For a new securities issue, the characteristics of the securities on offer: coupon, amount, maturity.

Thailand Securities Depository Company CSD for Thailand.

Thomson Report An electronic transaction reporting system for international equities on the London Stock Exchange operated by Thomson.

Tick size The value of a one-point movement in the contract price.

Tied agent An individual or business which only sells one company's products (such as life assurance) making no pretext of offering independent advice on all the products available.

Time deposit Deposit on an account held with a financial institution for a fixed term or with the understanding that the depositor can withdraw only by giving notice.

Time value The amount by which an option's premium exceeds its intrinsic value. Where an option has no intrinsic value the premium consists entirely of time value.

Tom-Next Money placed on the money market from tomorrow for repayment the day after.

Tom/Spot Week Money placed on the money market from tomorrow for repayment one week after (Tom/Spot Month).

TOREX Dealing system of the Toronto Stock Exchange.

Touch The best prices available for a stock on the stock market, looking at all market-makers.

Tracker fund See **Index Fund**.

Trade date The date on which a trade is made.

Trade guarantees Guarantees in place in a market which ensure that all compared or netted trades will be settled as compared regardless of a counterparty default.

Traded option An option which is traded on an exchange.

Tradepoint RIE established in 1995 as a rival to the London Stock Exchange. Uses an order-driven matching system.

Trader An individual who buys and sells securities with the objective of making short-term gains.

Trading permits These are issued by exchanges and give the holder the right to have one trader at any one time trading in the contract(s) to which the permit relates.

Transfer agent Agent appointed by a corporation to maintain records of stock and bond owners, to cancel and issue certificates and to resolve problems arising from lost, destroyed or stolen certificates.

Transfer form Document which owners of registered documents must sign when they sell the security. Not required where a book entry transfer system is in use.

Transparency The degree to which a market is characterized by prompt availability of accurate price and volume information which gives participants assurance that the market is fair.

TRAX Trade confirmation system for the Euro-markets operated by ISMA.

Treasury Arm of government responsible for all financial decisions and regulation of the financial services sector.

Treasury bill Money-market instrument issued with a life of less than one year issued by the US and UK governments.

Treasury bonds (US) US government bond issued with a 30-year maturity.

Treasury notes (US) US government bond issued with 2-, 3-, 5- and 7- year maturity.

Tri-party repo Repo which utilizes an intermediary custodian to oversee the exchange of securities and cash.

Triple A – rating The highest credit rating for a bond or company – the risk of default (or non-payment) is negligible.

Trustee Is appointed to oversee the management of certain funds. Responsible for ensuring that the fund is managed correctly and that the interests of the investor are protected and that all relevant regulations and legislation are complied with.

TSA Trading System for Amsterdam – the Dutch dealing system.

TSCD Taiwan Securities Central Depository.

Turn See **Spread**.

Turnaround Securities bought and sold for settlement on the same day.

Turnaround time The time available or needed to settle a turnaround trade.

Two-way price Simultaneous prices in a stock quoted by a market-maker, the lower at which he is willing to buy and the higher at which he is willing to sell.

Underlying asset The asset from which the future or option's price is derived.

Undersubscribed Circumstance when people have applied for fewer shares than are available in a new issue.

Underwriters Institutions which agree to take up shares in a new issue if it is undersubscribed. They will charge an underwriting fee.

Unit trust A system whereby money from a number of investors is pooled together and invested collectively on their behalf. Each owns a unit (or number of them) the value of which depends on the value of those items owned by the trust.

UNIVYC Clearing settlement and depository organization for the Czech market.

Unrealized profit Profit which has not arisen from a sale – an increase in value of an asset.

Up-and-in option A knock-in option where the trigger is higher than the underlying rate at the start. See **Down-and-in option; Up-and-out option; Down-and-out option**.

Up-and-out option A knock-out option where the trigger is higher than the underlying rate at the start. See **Up-and-in option; Down-and-in option; Down-and-out option**.

Value at risk (VaR) The maximum amount which a bank expects to lose, with a given confidence level, over a given time period.

Variation margin The process of revaluing an exchange traded product each day. It is the difference between the closing price on the previous day against the current closing price. It is physically paid or received each day by the clearing organization. It is often referred to as the mark-to-market.

Volatility The degree of scatter of the underlying price when compared to the mean average rate.

Vostro A vostro account is another bank's account held at our bank in our currency.

VPC Swedish Central Securities Depository (Värdepapper-centralen).

Warrant agent A bank appointed by the issuer as an intermediary between the issuing company and the (physical) warrant holders, interacting when the latter want to exercise the warrants.

Warrants An option which can be listed on an exchange, with a lifetime of generally more than one year.

Weekly Official Intelligence (WOI) Weekly publication by the London Stock Exchange which provides (among other things) a summary of company announcements during that week.

Withholding tax In the securities industry, a tax imposed by a government's tax authorities on dividends and interest paid.

Writer A person who has sold an open derivatives contract and is obliged to deliver or take delivery upon notification of exercise from the buyer.

XETRA Dealing system of the Deutsche Börse.

Yankee bond A US dollar bond issued in the USA by a non-USA corporation.

Yield Internal rate of return expressed as a percentage.

Yield curve For securities that expose the investor to the same credit risk, a graph showing the relationship at a given point in the time between yield and current maturity. Yield curves are typically drawn using yields on governments of various maturities.

Yield to maturity The rate of return yielded by a debt security held to maturity when both interest payments and the investor's capital gain or loss on the security are taken into account.

Zero coupon bond A bond issued with no coupon but a price substantially below par so that only capital is accrued over the life of the loan, and yield is comparable to coupon bearing instruments.

The contents of this glossary of terms have been compiled from reliable sources and are believed to be correct. However, Derivatives Management Services Ltd and Computer Based Learning Limited can take no responsibility whatsoever for any loss, claim or damages caused in whatever manner as a result of the reader using information taken from this work.

Index